August 25, 2021

all the best !

Enjoy my Cl

page 186.

Jeff Lane

D0661714

THE
13 STEPS TO
RICHES

Featuring Denis Waitley

#1 BESTSELLER

DESIRE
VOLUME 1

HABITUDE
WARRIOR

Orders by U.S. trade bookstores and wholesalers.
Email info@ BeyondPublishing.net

The Beyond Publishing Speakers Bureau can bring authors to your live event. For more information or to book an event contact the Beyond Publishing Speakers Bureau speak@BeyondPublishing.net

The Author can be reached directly at BeyondPublishing.net

Manufactured and printed in the United States of America distributed globally by BeyondPublishing.net

BEYOND
PUBLISHING

Library of Congress Control Number: 2021913544

ISBN hardcover: 978-1-63792-080-0

ISBN paperback: 978-1-63792-074-9

TESTIMONIALS
THE 13 STEPS TO RICHES

"What an honor to collaborate with so many personal development leaders from around the world as we Co-Author together honoring the amazing principles by Napoleon Hill in this new book series, *The 13 Steps to Riches*, by Habitude Warrior and Erik "Mr. Awesome" Swanson. Well done "Mr. Awesome" for putting together such an amazing series. If you want to up-level your life, read every book in this series and learn to apply each of these time-tested steps and principles."

Denis Waitley ~ Author of *Psychology of Winning & The NEW Psychology of Winning* - Top Qualities of a 21st Century Winner

"Just as *Think and Grow Rich* reveals the 13 steps to success discovered by Napoleon Hill after interviewing the richest people around the world (and many who considered themselves failures) in the early 1900's, *The 13 Steps to Riches*, produced by Habitude Warrior and Erik Swanson takes a modern look at those same 13 steps. It brings together many of today's personal development leaders to share their stories of how the 13 Steps to Riches have created and propelled their own successes. I am honored to participate and share the power of Faith in my life. If you truly want to accelerate reaching the success you deserve, read every volume of *The 13 Steps to Riches*."

Sharon Lechter ~ 5 Time N.Y. Times Best-Selling Author. Author of *Think and Grow Rich for Women*, Co-Author of *Exit Rich, Rich Dad Poor Dad, Three Feet from Gold, Outwitting the Devil* and *Success and Something Greater* ~ SharonLechter.com

"The most successful book on personal achievement ever written is now being elaborated upon by many of the world's top thought leaders. I'm honored to Co-Author this series on the amazing principles from Napoleon Hill, in *The 13 Steps to Riches,* by Habitude Warrior and Erik "Mr. Awesome" Swanson."

> *Jim Cathcart* ~ Best-Selling Author of *Relationship Selling* and *The Acorn Principle,* among many others. Certified Speaking Professional (CSP) and Former President of the National Speakers Association (NSA)

"Where else can you find 13 leaders sharing their amazing insights and principles of success, while honoring one of the best books ever published in *Think and Grow Rich* by Napoleon Hill? I know... right here! Pick up your copy of *The 13 Steps to Riches* book series and follow these time-tested steps and principles that will change your life if you take action on them."

> *Steve Sims* ~ N. Y. Times Best-Selling Author of *Bluefishing -The Art of Making Things Happen*

"How exciting to team up with the amazing Habitude Warrior community of leaders such as Erik Swanson, Sharon Lechter, John Assaraf, Denis Waitley and so many more transformational and self-help icons to bring you these timeless and proven concepts in the fields of success and wealth. *The 13 Steps to Riches* book series will help you reach your dreams and accomplish your goals faster than you have ever experienced before!"

> *Marie Diamond* ~ Featured in *The Secret,* Modern Day Spiritual Teacher, Inspirational Speaker, Feng Shui Master

"If you are looking to crystalize your mightiest dream, rekindle your passion, breakthrough limiting beliefs and learn from those who have done exactly what you want to do - read this book! In this transformational masterpiece, *The 13 Steps to Riches*, self-development guru Erik Swanson has collected the sage wisdom and time tested truths from subject matter experts and amalgamated it into a one-stop-shop resource library that will change your life forever!"

Dan Clark ~ Speaker Hall of Fame & N. Y. Times Best-Selling Author of *The Art of Significance*

"Life has always been about who you surround yourself with. I am in excellent company with this collaboration from my fellow authors and friends, paying tribute to the life changing principles by Napoleon Hill in this amazing new book series, *The 13 Steps to Riches*, organized by Habitude Warrior's founder and my dear friend, Erik Swanson. Hill said, 'Your big opportunity may be right where you are now.' This book series is a must-read for anyone who wants to change their life and prosper, starting now."

Alec Stern ~ America's Startup Success Expert, Co-Founder of Constant Contact

"Success leaves clues and the Co-Authors in this awesome book series, *The 13 Steps to Riches*, will continue the Napoleon Hill legacy with tools, tips and modern-day principals that greatly expand on the original masterpiece... *Think and Grow Rich*. If you are serious about living your life to the max, get this book series now!

John Assaraf ~ Chairman/CEO NeuroGym, MrNeuroGym.com, N. Y. Times Best-Selling Author of *Having It All, Innercise,* and *The Answer*. Also featured in *The Secret*

"Napoleon Hill had a tremendous impact on my consciousness when I was very young – there were very few books nor the type of trainings that we see today to lead us to success. Whenever you have the opportunity to read and harness *The 13 Steps to Riches* as they are presented in this series, be happy (and thankful) that there were many of us out there applying the principles, testing the teachings, making the mistakes, and now being offered to you in a way that they are clear, simple and concise – with samples and distinctions that will make it easier for you to design a successful life which includes adding value to others, solving world problems, and making the world work for 100% of humanity... Read on... those dreams are about to come true!"

Doria Cordova ~ CEO of Money & You, Excellerated Business School, Global Business Developer, Ambassador of New Education

"Over the years, I have been blessed with many rare and amazing opportunities to invest my time and energy. These opportunities require a keen eye and immediate action. This is one of those amazing opportunities for you as a reader! I highly recommend you pick up every book in this series of The 13 Steps to Riches by Habitude Warrior and Erik Swanson! Learn from modern day leaders who have embraced the lessons from the great Napoleon Hill in his classic book from 1937, Think and Grow Rich."

Kevin Harrington ~ Original "Shark" on Shark Tank, Creator of the Infomercial, Pioneer of the As Seen on TV brand, Co-Author of *Mentor to Millions*

"When you begin your journey, you will quickly learn of the importance of the first step of The 13 Steps To Riches. A burning desire is the start of all worthwhile achievements. Erik 'Mr. Awesome' Swanson's newest book series contains a wealth of assistance to make your journey both successful and enjoyable. Start today... because tomorrow is not guaranteed on your calendar."

Don Green ~ 45 Years of Banking, Finance & Entrepreneurship, Best-Selling Author of *Everything I know About Success I Learned From Napoleon Hill & Napoleon Hill My Mentor: Timeless Principles to Take Your Success to the Next Level & Your Millionaire Mindset*

NAPOLEON HILL

I would like to personally acknowledge and thank the one and only Napoleon Hill for his work, dedication, and most importantly believing in himself. His unwavering belief in himself, whether he realized this or not, had been passed down from generation to generation to millions and millions of individuals across this planet including me!

I'm sure, at first, as many of us experience throughout our lives as well, he most likely had his doubts. Think about it. Being offered to work for Andrew Carnegie for a full 20 years with zero pay and no guarantee of success had to be a daunting decision. But, I thank you for making that decision years and years ago. It paved the path for countless many who have trusted in themselves and found success in their own rights. You gave us all hope and desire to bank on the most important entity in our world today - ourselves!

For this, I thank you Sir, from the bottom of my heart and the top of all of our bank accounts. Let us all follow the 13 Steps to Riches and prosper in so many areas of our lives.

~ Erik "Mr Awesome" Swanson

JOHN CHARLES SWANSON

I would like to dedicate our series of The 13 Steps to Riches to my Father! He taught me so many lessons throughout my life. One of the main lessons he instilled in me from an early age was to never, ever give up! He coupled this lesson with the commitment to always helping and serving mankind. This is where my motto came from, which I live to the fullest each and every day. That motto is: "NDSO!" No Drama - Serve Others! Thanks Dad! I love you and will see you one day again. I love you always!

~ Your Son, Erik

CONTENTS

FOREWORD

by Sharon Lechter

In 1908, a young Napoleon Hill was charged with researching the steps to success by Andrew Carnegie, the richest man in the world at the time. Carnegie introduced Hill to many of his successful friends including Thomas Edison, Henry Ford, and many other millionaires of his generation so he could organize the world's first philosophy of personal achievement. Twenty-five years later, in 1937, Napoleon Hill released *Think and Grow Rich,* which is still considered today as the quintessential thesis on success.

Why? Because it was not one man's philosophy but derived from Hill interviewing 500 of the most successful men at the time and many more who considered themselves failures. The book reveals tried and true steps to success that are as true today as they were when the book was released in 1937.

Just as *Think and Grow Rich* reveals the 13 steps to success that Hill discovered, this series of books called *The 13 Steps to Riches*, produced by Habitude Warrior and Erik Swanson honors Napoleon Hill and his wisdom by taking a modern look at those same 13 steps. Our authors share their stories of how the 13 Steps to Riches have created and propelled their own successes.

In honor of Napoleon Hill, allow me to take you through those 13 Steps and highlight the importance of each one in his own words.

1. Burning Desire

"Wishing will not bring riches. But desiring riches with a state of mind that becomes an obsession, then planning definite ways and means to acquire riches, and backing those plans with persistence which does not recognize failure, will bring riches."
– Napoleon Hill

2. Faith

"Faith is the starting point of all accumulation of riches... Riches begin in the form of thought! The amount is limited only by the person in whose mind the thought is put into motion. Faith removes limitations!" – Napoleon Hill

3. Auto-Suggestion

"No thought, whether it is negative or positive, can enter the subconscious mind without the aid of the principle of auto-suggestion. Your ability to use the principle of auto-suggestion will depend, very largely, upon your capacity to concentrate upon a given desire until that desire becomes a burning obsession." – Napoleon Hill

4. Specialized Knowledge

"Successful men, in all callings, never stop acquiring specialized knowledge related to their major purpose, business, or profession. Those who are not successful usually make the mistake of believing that the knowledge-acquiring period ends when one finishes school." – Napoleon Hill

5. Imagination

"Ideas are the beginning points of all fortunes. Ideas are products of the imagination ... Man's only limitation, within reason, lies in his development and use of his imagination." – Napoleon Hill

"Whoever you are, wherever you may live, whatever occupation you may be engaged in, just remember in the future, every time you see the words 'Coca-Cola,' that its vast empire of wealth and influence grew out of a single idea." – Napoleon Hill

6. Organized Planning

"Opportunity has spread its wares before you. Step up to the front, select what you want, create your plan, put the plan into action, and follow through with persistence ... Most of us are good "starters" but poor "finishers" of everything we begin. Moreover, people are prone to give up at the first signs of defeat. There is no substitute for persistence." – Napoleon Hill

7. Decision

"The man of decision cannot be stopped! The man of indecision cannot be started! Take your own choice...
People who fail to accumulate money, without exception, have the habit of reaching decisions, if at all, very slowly, and of changing these decisions quickly and often." – Napoleon Hill

8. Persistence

"Patience, persistence and perspiration make an unbeatable combination for success...Riches do not respond to wishes. They respond only to definite plans, backed by definite desires, through constant persistence." – Napoleon Hill

9. Power of the Master Mind

"No individual may have great power without availing himself of the "Master Mind" ... A group of brains coordinated (or connected) in a spirit of harmony will provide more thought-energy than a single brain, just as a group of electric batteries will provide more energy than a single battery." – Napoleon Hill

10. The Mystery of Sex Transmutation

"Sex desire is the most powerful of human desires. When driven by this desire, men develop keenness of imagination, courage, willpower, persistence, and creative ability unknown to them at other times. Love, romance, and sex are all emotions capable of driving men to heights of super achievement. When combined, these three emotions may lift one to an altitude of genius." – Napoleon Hill

11. The Subconscious Mind

"The subconscious mind will not remain idle! If you fail to plant desires in your subconscious mind, it will feed upon the thoughts which reach it as the result of your neglect. Positive and negative emotions cannot occupy the mind at the same time. One or the other must dominate. It is your responsibility to make sure that positive emotions constitute the dominating influence of your mind." – Napoleon Hill

12. The Brain

"You have a brain and a mind of your own. Use it, and reach your own decisions…Every human brain is capable of picking up vibrations of thought which are being released by other brains … The Creative Imagination is the "receiving set" of the brain, which receives thoughts released by the brains of others." – Napoleon Hill

13. The Sixth Sense

"Through the aid of the sixth sense, you will be warned of impending dangers in time to avoid them, and notified of opportunities in time to embrace them. This is especially true if your major purpose is that of accumulation of money or other material things. The chapter on the sixth sense was included, because the book is designed for the purpose of presenting a complete philosophy by which individuals may unerringly guide themselves in attaining whatever they ask of life." – Napoleon Hill

Napoleon Hill knew that all great success begins with a burning desire. This burning desire creates passion which becomes the fuel to turn our dreams into reality. This fuel turns into commitment which becomes action toward our goals. Get clear about what you want and why you want it. Commit yourself to taking the actions to pursue the life you want. By following these 13 Steps you will place yourself in the position of greatest potential to realize the success that you so richly deserve.

I read and study *Think and Grow Rich* every year. Even though the book doesn't change... I do. Each time I read it I find something perfect for my current situation (often something I don't remember being there before). As we come together in this series of books it is to honor the impact Napoleon Hill has had on our lives and to share that impact with you so that you can find exactly what you need today. Study each volume and find the fuel to propel you forward to reach the success you so richly deserve.

To your success,

Sharon Lechter

Author of *Think and Grow Rich for Women*
Co-author of *Three Feet From Gold, Outwitting the Devil, Success and Something Greater, Rich Dad Poor Dad* and 14 other Rich Dad books.

www.SharonLechter.com

INTRODUCTION

by Don Green

ERIK SWANSON & DON GREEN

Once you give yourself the gift of reading Erik Swanson's newest book series, *The 13 Steps to Riches*, you are sure to realize why he has earned his nickname, *"Mr. Awesome."* Readers usually read books for two reasons – they want to be entertained or they want to improve their knowledge in a certain subject. Mr. Awesome's new book series will help you do both.

I urge you to not only read this great book series in it's entirety, but also apply the principles held within into your our life. Use the experience Erik Swanson has gained to reach your own level of success. I highly encourage you to invest in yourself by reading self-help materials, such as *The 13 Steps to Riches*, and I truly know you will discover that it will be one of the best investments you could ever make.

Don Green
Executive Director and CEO
The Napoleon Hill Foundation

Denis Waitley

MOTIVATION BY DESIRE

Positive self-motivation is the inner drive that keeps you moving forward in pursuit of your goals. Winners in every field in the game of life are driven by desire. There never has been a consistent winner in any profession who didn't have that burning desire to win…internalized. Although the Scriptures have preached it as a basic axiom in life for centuries, this concept was first presented in the self-improvement industry by Earl Nightingale in his platinum audio recording of *The Strangest Secret*. The strangest secret is that we become what we think about most of the time. In other words, we and our children are motivated every day and moved by our current dominant thoughts. We are moved in the direction of what we dwell on. We can't concentrate on the reverse of an idea. Everyone in life is self-motivated, positively or negatively. Even a decision to do nothing is a decision based on motivation.

In the field of psychology, we make a basic distinction between intrinsic and extrinsic motivation. Having intrinsic motivation means doing something for its own sake, like playing a sport just for the joy of playing. On the other hand, extrinsic motivation pulls you by the power of some external benefit or tangible reward you'll attain by taking action, as in the case of a professional athlete who plays primarily for money, rather than for the fun or challenge of the sport. It also influences people in their business careers, especially among those who are driven fundamentally by the income they receive, rather than by the love of the service they provide.

Motivation is a highly emotional state, and the great physical and mental motivators in life, such as survival and love, are filled with emotion. And the two key emotions which dominate all human motivation, with opposite, but nearly equally effective results, are fear and desire. Fear, of course, is the most powerful, negative motivator of all. Fear is the great dictator that forces us to do things that we feel we have to do because of the consequences. Fear is the great inhibitor, the red light that tells us that we can't do things because of the obstacles and risks.

Through the years, I've been telling the story of a man who may unwittingly have become a victim of his own negative premonition, a kind of self-inflicted voodoo spell. It was a true account of a man named Nick Sitzman, a strong, healthy individual who worked as a yardman for a railroad company in Omaha, Nebraska. According to his supervisor, Nick was a good worker who got along fine with his fellow workers and was reliable on the job. He had one noticeable fault, however. He was a notorious worrier. He was cynical about everything and usually feared the worst about the world situation, the economy, the weather and the future, in general.

One summer day, the train crews were informed that they could quit an hour early, in honor of the foreman's birthday. Accidentally, Nick was locked in an empty, isolated refrigerator boxcar that was in the yard for repairs. He had been working in it when the rest of the workmen left the site. Nick panicked. He banged and shouted until his fists were raw and his voice hoarse. No one paid any attention. If they heard him, they associated the sound with a playground nearby or with the noise of other trains backing in and out of the yard.

Hey, let me out of here, it must be zero degrees in this refrigerator car, he must have thought. *If I can't get out soon, I'll freeze to death.* He found a cardboard box and, shivering uncontrollably, he scrawled this message to his wife and family: "So cold, body is getting numb. If I could just go to sleep. These may be my last words."

The next morning, the crew slid open the heavy doors of the boxcar and found Nick dead. An autopsy revealed that every physical sign in his body indicated he had frozen to death. But the irony was that the refrigeration unit was inoperative, and there was plenty of fresh air in the boxcar. It was a mild summer afternoon and evening, with the temperature inside steady at about sixty-one degrees. His fear motivation became a self-fulfilling prophecy.

As a positive power, belief becomes the promise of the realization of things hoped for and unseen. As a negative power, it is the premonition of our deepest fears and unseen darkness. A self-fulfilling prophecy perhaps can be best defined as a statement or concept that is not necessarily true nor false, but is capable of becoming true if it is believed and internalized.

Desire is like a strong, positive magnet. It beckons and welcomes us toward our goals. Fear usually looks through the rearview mirror at missed opportunities and problems and with apprehension to the future.

Fear breeds compulsion. Desire creates positive propulsion. Fear breeds inhibition. Desire triggers ignition power. Winners have learned how to concentrate on the desired results, rather than possible problems. And winners dwell on the rewards of success, instead of the penalties of failure.

The Law of Attraction Takes Action

Over a decade ago, I participated in the video and book project called *The Secret*, based upon the Law of Attraction. One way or another, our actions cause rewards and consequences. "To every action," as Sir Isaac Newton observed, "there is always an equal and opposite reaction." Good begets good, and evil leads to more evil. This is one of the Universe's eternal, fundamental truths, which I have referred to as The Unfailing Boomerang or the Law of Cause and Effect.

It means that every cause (action) will create an effect (reaction) approximately equal in intensity. Making good use of our minds, skills, and talents will bring positive rewards in our outer lives. Assuming the personal responsibility to make the best use of our talents and time will result in an enormous gain in happiness, success, and wealth. This is true of everyone.

The truly successful winners, those who have built financial empires or accomplished great deeds for society, are those who have taken personal responsibility to heart and to soul. By being true to themselves and others, they achieve success, wealth, and inner happiness. In the end, we, ourselves—far more than any outsider—are the people with the greatest ability to steal our own time, talents, and accomplishments.

I'm fond of a story from the Old Testament Book of Leviticus about a sacred ceremony called "The Escaped Goat." When the people's troubles became overwhelming in those early days, a healthy male goat was led into the temple. The tribe's highest priest placed his hand on the animal's head and solemnly recited the long list of the people's woes. Then the goat was released—and it ran off, supposedly taking the human troubles and evil spirits with him. That was some four thousand years ago, but the concept of the scapegoat remains in full force today. Blaming someone else or something else for our problems is nearly as old as civilization—and stays consistently young. When Adam ate of the apple, he quickly pointed at Eve. "The woman you've put here with me made me do it," he said.

We live in a land of incredible abundance. Americans enjoy material riches and a civic and legal inheritance that people of other countries continue to die for. We protest for individual liberty and social order in the same breath. We strive for material wealth, hoping that spiritual riches will come with it as a bonus. We plead for more protection from crime, but demand less interference in our social habits. We want to cut taxes and build our own empires—at the same time, we want our government to provide more financial security. But we can't have it both ways. If we want results, we must pay the price.

Life's greatest risk is depending on others for your security, which can really come only by planning, acting, and making choices that will make you independent.

There was a very cautious man,

Who never laughed or played;

He never risked, he never tried,

He never sang or prayed.

And when he one day passed away,

His insurance was denied;

For since he really never lived,

They claimed he never died.

There are two primary choices in our lives: to accept conditions as they exist or to assume the responsibility for changing them. The price of success includes taking responsibility for giving up bad habits and invalid assumptions; setting a worthy example in our own lives; leading ourselves and others down a new and unfamiliar path; working more to reach a goal and being willing to delay gratification along the way; distancing ourselves from a peer group that isn't helping us succeed and therefore tends or wants to hold us back; and being willing to face criticism and jealousy from people who would like to keep us stuck in place with them.

My decades of research have convinced me that the happiest, best-adjusted individuals in their present and older lives are those who believe they have a strong measure of control over their lives. They seem to choose more appropriate responses to what occurs and to stand up to inevitable changes with less apprehension. They learn from their past mistakes, rather than replay them. They spend time "doing" in the present, rather than fearing what may happen. So, stop stewing and start doing. If the pandemic has taught us anything, it is that we must be prepared for sudden change and surprises on a daily basis. Being resilient in turbulent times is our new reality.

Action TNT: Today not Tomorrow

My grandfather owned a bookstore and bindery in San Diego, where I used to work on weekends as a pre-teen and teenager. In addition to gluing books together and sweeping out his store, I loved browsing and sampling the stacks of books on the shelves. It was like a candy store of wisdom to me. He had a poster on the wall that I copied in my notebook, because my grandpa said it was an important lesson for me to learn when I was young. He said procrastination is a favorite hiding place for people who are afraid to risk making mistakes, which is why he almost never put off any important decisions regarding the family. I have memorized that poster and refer to it often when I spend time puttering, majoring in minors and doing meaningless activities that are tension-relieving, instead of goal-achieving. The title is simply "Tomorrow."

He was going to be that he wanted to be –tomorrow. None would be kinder and braver than he –tomorrow. A friend who was troubled and weary he knew, who'd be glad for a lift and needed it too, on him he would call and see what he could do –tomorrow. Each morning, he'd stack up the letters he'd write –tomorrow. And thought of the clients he'd fill with delight – tomorrow. But he hadn't a minute to stop on his way, "More time I will give to others," he'd say –"tomorrow." The greatest of leaders this man would have been – tomorrow. The world would have hailed him had he ever seen – tomorrow. But in fact, he passed on, and he faded from view. And all that he left here when his life was through, was a mountain of things he intended to do – TOMORROW.

Motivation into Motive-Action

Here are some motivation actions you can take to reach your goals, instead of letting fear and negativity keep you in a constant state of frustration and anxiety.

Remember, we become what we think about. What the mind harbors, the body manifests in some way. Focus your mind (which I call your software program) on your desired goals that you want your brain and body (your hard-drive and hardware) to achieve.

View failure as target correction. Failure is only a detour, not a dead end. The person interested in success has to learn to view failure as a healthy, inevitable part of the process of getting to the top. I look at failure as the fertilizer of success. Don't roll in it. Use the experience as growth material. So, make a pact with yourself. I suggest you write an agreement with yourself. Promise that you won't allow a failure to be more than a learning experience that allows you to move more quickly to the place you want to be.

Keep your self-talk affirmative. Whether you're at work, at home, or on the golf course or tennis court, your subconscious is recording every word. Instead of "should have," say "will do." Instead of "if only," say "next time." Instead of "Yes, but…," say "Why not?" Instead of "problem," say "opportunity." Instead of "difficult," say "challenging." Instead of "could have," say "my goal." Instead of "someday," say "today." Say, "In the hole" before you putt on the green while playing golf, and "first serve in" when it's your serve on the tennis court.

Forget perfection. Only the saints are perfect—and "Sainthood is acceptable only in saints." Accept the flaws and count your blessings, instead of your blemishes.

1. Declare a moratorium on negatives—negative thoughts, negative people, negative forms of entertainment. Keep your desire to succeed strong by erasing thoughts of the downside. To win, you must continuously motivate yourself toward your goals. And you must be willing to do this yourself.

2. Be willing to say to yourself, "I'm on the right road. I'm doing okay. I'm succeeding." We too frequently become adept at identifying our flaws and failures. Become equally adept at recognizing your achievements. What are you doing now that you weren't doing one month ago … six months ago … a year ago? What habits have changed? Chart your progress. Doing well once or twice is relatively easy. Real winning is *continuously* moving ahead. Winning is tough, in part, because it is so easy to revert to old habits and former lifestyles. Over the long run, you need to give yourself regular feedback and monitor your performance. Reinforce yourself positively to stay on track. Don't wait for an award ceremony, promotion, friend or mentor to show appreciation for your work. Do it yourself! Do it now. Take pride in your own efforts on a daily basis.

3. Set up a dynamic daily routine. Getting into a positive routine or groove, instead of a negative rut, will help you become more effective. Why is the subway the most energy-efficient means of transportation? Because it runs on a track. Think of the order in your day, instead of the routine. Don't worry

about sameness, neatness, or everything exactly in its place. Order is being able to do what you really choose and not taking on more than you can manage. Order frees you up. Get into the swing of a healthy, daily routine and discover how much more control you'll gain in your life.

Here are 5 keys to adding order to a winning routine:

1. Simplify – challenge complicated plans or processes.

2. Don't spend a lot of time searching for things – you probably don't need them anyway.

3. Do what you promise to do – and promise only what you can do.

4. Set effective agendas with others ahead of time – so neither of you is disappointed.

5. Monitor yourself – in order to make sure you accomplish what you set out to do.

And remember: change your attitude and lifestyle, and many of your outcomes will change automatically. Because you are an uncut gemstone of priceless value. Cut and polish your potential with knowledge, skills, and service, and you will be in great demand throughout your life. Optimists rule the future. Imagination and innovation flourish when nations, companies, teams, families, and individuals are motivated by the rewards of success, instead of the penalties of failure. Fear compels and inhibits. Desire is that burning fire of hope within that turns dreams into reality. Ask any athlete training for 1,200 days for an opportunity to be an Olympian, what motivates her or him. It is the torch of passion.

DENIS WAITLEY

About Denis Waitley: Denis Waitley has inspired, informed, challenged and entertained audiences for over 25 years from the boardrooms of multi-national corporations to the locker rooms of world-class athletes and in the meeting rooms of thousands of conventioneers throughout the world. Recently, he was voted business speaker of the year by the Sales and Marketing Executives Association and by Toastmasters International and inducted into the International Speakers Hall of Fame.

With over 10 million audio programs sold in 14 languages, Denis Waitley is one of the most listened-to voices on personal and career success. He is the author of 16 non-fiction books, including several International best sellers, *Seeds of Greatness, Being the Best, The Winners' Edge, The Joy of Working,* and *Empire of the Mind.*

His audio album, *The Psychology of Winning* is the all-time best selling program on self-mastery.

Denis Waitley has studied and counseled winners in every field from Apollo astronauts to Super Bowl champions, from sales achievers to government leaders and youth groups.

During the 1980's, he served as Chairman of Psychology on the U.S. Olympic Committee's Sports Medicine Council, responsible for performance enhancement of all U.S. Olympic athletes.

Denis Waitley is a founding director of the National Council on Self-Esteem and the President's Council on Vocational Education, and recently received the "Youth Flame Award" from the National Council on Youth Leadership for his outstanding contribution to high school youth leadership.

As President of the International Society for Advanced Education, inspired by Dr. Jonea Salk, he counseled returning POW's from Vietnam and conducted simulation and stress management seminars for Apollo astronauts.

Author's Website: *www.DenisWaitley.com*
Book Series Website & Author's Bio: *www.The13StepstoRiches.com*

Erik "Mr. Awesome" Swanson

DESIRE IS A LIFE'S JOURNEY

The late, great Dr. Napoleon Hill wrote in his amazing masterpiece from 1937 *Think and Grow Rich* that desire is the starting point of all achievement! I 1,000 percent agree with him. I would take it one step further and say that desire is and should be included in the journey, as well as the finish line, of all achievement, and you should even allow it to catapult you to the next desire, to up-level you as an awesome human being on this planet! What an absolute honor it is to be able to learn and follow in the steps of such leaders in my journey in the world of personal development.

My definition of desire has changed over the many years from when I started tapping into it about twenty-four years ago. At first, I believed desire was all about what I wanted to accomplish. For me, it was an internal dialogue that included only myself. It consisted of the accomplishments of my personal goals in life. Although utilizing desire is a fantastic way to improve my personal life, I soon started to see that it was not all about me. Now, my true definition of desire is one that helps the world and everyone around me. It's a burning, internal, awesome, goal strategy with a commitment to never give up on my mission to assist people around me to up-level their lives for the better. Life is a team sport. Let's get in this game together.

Desire shows up in so many areas of our lives. I recall the very first time I had a glimpse of the concept of desire. It included seven letters, starting with the letter "k," and ending with my five-year-old heart pounding. It was my first day of kindergarten. She walked by me as we were putting our little lunch boxes in the cubby holes. Her name was Kirsten! Wow! I was in love! She had such long, golden hair, like an angel, and a smile to match. I'm not sure if she noticed that every few days, I would sit closer and closer to her until I finally was right next to her in class. Ahhhh, heaven! I finally made it. Now, I just need to muster up enough courage to speak to her. Oops, naptime already? Okay, well, I guess I'll strike up a conversation after we take a little nap together.

Now, I would love to tell you that the conversation went very smoothly. You know, "So, what's an angel like you doing in kindergarten?" ... or like some cool line like that I threw her way. Nope. That wasn't the case. I think my very first words to her were something like, "Your choice of crayon color is impeccable." She smiled and just walked away.

Okay, I vow to myself from here on out, I will kiss this beautiful angel, Kirsten, by the end of the school year. I'm committed! Nothing is going to get in my way... not even me. It's my very first desire and goal that I remember setting for myself as a little human being.

Fast-forward to my senior year of high school. When every one of my friends knew where they were going to go to college the following year, I still struggled with my decision. Or, should I say that my grades helped me struggle with the decision. I was so determined to go to the same university that all of my friends were going to, yet, my grades were determined to place me elsewhere.

As I was pondering what to do, my best friend in school suggested that I become friends with one of the jocks in my high school, simply because his father was the actual dean of the university I was desiring to attend. Okay, mission set! Desire on! I'm ready. Now what? I didn't technically have a plan of action. But, what I did have was the burning desire to never quit, and I innately realized that what's "inside of me" would determine what's "in my outside reality." Dr. Napoleon Hill teaches us that "Desire outwits Mother Nature" and to have a "Definite of Purpose." I decided to use these principles and GO FOR IT, NO MATTER WHAT! *I mean, what do I have to lose?* I thought.

So, off I went to find this jock and become friends with him. It worked! I simply found common ground with him in something he was interested in. That interest turned out to be downhill skiing. Great… I'm *not* a skier. But, I'll tell you what. I was a skier for as long as it took to win his friendship over. It worked!

Because of my tenacity and determination to complete my current mission of desire, I got accepted to my school of choice and went to the university with all my friends. Of course, with a little—or should I say a lot—of help from my new jock friend and his pull with his father. Never allow yourself to give up on yourself! You deserve greatness, and greatness is simply on the other side of your determination, commitment, and action to your goals and desires.

After university and a few years of trying to figure out what I wanted to do with my life, I was introduced to a brilliant mind. He was apparently very well-known as one of the main leaders on the planet for personal development, sales, and management training. After I asked around and started to hear his name over and over again from those I admired in very successful businesses, I started to set a goal to work with him. Not only work with him, but become one of his very best trainers. Not only become one of his best trainers, but actually share stages with him around the world. This man I'm referring to is the one and only Brian Tracy!

Would you like to know a secret? If you ever desire to work with someone who is brilliant, but who you feel is untouchable and out of reach to you, start studying his or her work. Start applying his or her work and teachings into your everyday habits. Start surrounding yourself with his or her thoughts, and soon, the Universe will reward you for your burning desire! This is exactly what I did. I figured that if I could positively "brainwash" myself with all of Brian Tracy's great teachings and habits, then I could become someone like him and ultimately reach the success he did.

In one of my other books, *Crush and Dominate*, I teach a concept called "Copy, Don't Copy." It's simply the concept of training yourself to think, act, and grow like the mentors you desire to be like, but still being authentically you. You can use this concept in any area of your life. It doesn't have to be just in business. Ultimately, I became an International Senior Trainer with my mentor, Brian Tracy, and traveled the world working with him for about ten years. This changed my life! Or should I say, "I changed my life!" You can, too. You simply need to make that commitment and realize that nothing is out of your reach, as long as you believe in the concept of having a "burning desire."

Looking back at the journey of my life as it pertains to how important this concept of desire truly is, I would have to say that although I was utilizing the concept, I never fully understood the true meaning. Yes, I conquered tons of goals that I thought were part of my own burning desires. But, as I mentioned at the beginning of this conversation, I have come to realize lately that it's not all about ourselves. A true "burning desire" to me is all about helping the world and everyone on this planet.

Take, for example, this book series. I could have easily written all of these chapters by myself about my journey and how I grew from each of the 13 Steps to Riches. But, it's *not* all about me. It's about how "WE" as a collective group of *awesome* individuals make up an amazing team to go further by helping each other grow. This is how we, as a team, can help others grow as well. This series you are about to embark upon—and hopefully, embrace—will give you a modern day's journey from people from around the world who use these amazing 13 Steps to Riches principles in their lives, while dealing with struggles, adversities, and triumphs. This is "OUR" journey together. I truly hope you enjoy it and join us!

Oh, and if you are still wondering if I ever ended up kissing my kindergarten crush, Kirsten, you will simply have to read our next book in the series to find out.

ERIK SWANSON

About Erik "Mr. Awesome" Swanson: As an award-winning International Keynote Speaker and 10 Time #1 International Best-Selling Author, Erik "Mr. Awesome" Swanson is in great demand around the world! He speaks to an average of more than one million people per year, and he has been honored to have been invited to speak to the business and entrepreneurial school of Harvard University, as well as joining the Ted Talk Family with his latest TEDx speech called "A Dose of Awesome."

Erik has created and developed the super-popular Habitude Warrior Conference, which has a two-year waiting list and includes 33 top named speakers from around the world. It is a 'Ted Talk' style event which has quickly climbed to one of the top 10 events not to miss in the United States! He is the creator, founder, and CEO of the Habitude Warrior Mastermind and Global Speakers Mastermind. Erik is also one of the producers of *SpeakUP TV*, a show on Amazon Prime Video. His motto is clear... "NDSO!": No Drama — Serve Others!

Author's Website: *www.SpeakerErikSwanson.com*
Book Series Website & Author's Bio: *www.The13StepstoRiches.com*

BELIEVING DESIRES INTO EXISTENCE

"Without belief, definite purpose, and persistence, a desire becomes a mere wish."

Imagine being the type of person who obtains everything you've ever desired. Only the GREAT ONES, the RELENTLESS FEW, and the OBSESSED receive everything they want. My generation calls this G.O.A.T. (Greatest of All-Time). Whatever reference you may call it, a desire is a dream worth pursuing, and there should be no possible option for a cowardly retreat.

I'll share with you how you, too, can receive everything you want. I have invested a significant amount of time and study into the principles of success and steps to riches. I believe Three Incontestable Attributes coincide with the code of desire, and I wish to teach and champion these attributes through my life stories. Those attributes are: dreaming, believing, and having a definite purpose.

"DREAMS ARE THE SEEDLINGS OF REALITY."
-Napoleon Hill, Think and Grow Rich

As a young boy, I was extremely fond of watching the Olympics on television. When I watched athletes compete in the track and field events, I envisioned myself running just as fast. Because I desired and believed I could, it became my reality. I could outrun and outlast my siblings, parents, friends, and even other athletes older than I was.

Notably, as a young child, I wanted to experience myself being as quick as the track stars on T.V. So, I grabbed my sister's silky nighty from the laundry, which resembled sort of what the Olympians were wearing, slipped it on, and sped throughout the house and yard, orating the sounds made by airplanes and vehicles. Of course, my family thought I was silly, and my father worried for his firstborn son who was wearing his daughter's nighty and sprinting about the neighborhood. But in my vision, I was spectacular. For all I knew, I was superhuman freaky fast. Combining my desire for quickness and agility, my early fascination for airplanes, and my name being Jon Jr.–J.J. for short–I was awarded the nickname "J.J. the Jet."

Believing

Believing is living with a surety that what you dream of exists. Desire must be a belief–not merely a wish. Believing in my desire to be fast almost instantly made me fast, without any additional practice or enhancement. It was as if I could magically run faster than anyone on the playgrounds of elementary school. I dreamed so hard and saw myself as a strong and fast kid. I believed I was freaky-fast; therefore, I was freaky fast. I went from average kid to most highly favored and competitive in all recess games. Even if other kids kept up with me, I could find it within myself to turn up another gear and put on the jets–the J.J. jets.

My beliefs were selective—grades, reading, writing, and other essential matters weren't amongst the top dream and belief list; however, my desires were backed by beliefs, which became my reality. My desires made both physical and mental transformations within me.

Definite Purpose

Napoleon Hill said in Think and Grow Rich, "There is one quality which one must possess to win, and that is DEFINITENESS OF PURPOSE, the knowledge of what one wants, and a burning DESIRE to possess it." You've got to want something bad enough to get it, and anyone can.

My desire to be the fastest and most athletic person was severely challenged the older I grew. I wasn't always a gifted athlete. I honestly had to work for everything I ever did achieve. Other athletes whom I competed against were bigger, stronger, and quicker off the starting blocks. I always worked double-time and put in the extra effort to do my best and to compete at the top. I was always the first and last person at practices.

In 2007, my teammates and I traveled to Pocatello, Idaho, to compete in the Indoor National Track and Field competition. We had formed a relay team for the 4 x 800-meter relay race. Unfortunately, we were going into this race as complete underdogs, and I had a lot of ground to make up since my teammates weren't nearly as fast or in shape as I was. Our competition included the nationally ranked team from New York, our arch-rival high school from my hometown, and the nation's top 10 ranked relay teams.

Boom! The gun fired, and the race began. My other three teammates ran decent legs and kept us still competitively in the mix. I was handed the last baton and needed to catch our team up to place in the top 10. I utilized the tight wooden track corners to bust through groups of runners like I was a linebacker driving through the offensive line to tackle the running back in football. It was aggressive, probably illegal in the sport of track and field, and I was determined. I only had one definite purpose, and that was to catch up and pass as many people as I could. If you're as determined as I was, you push through all pain and go after what it is you want–you have a definite purpose. The circumstances were right, and my options were limited.

I turned the jets on–the J.J. jets–and made my move around the final lap to sprint to the finish line. I pushed through some excruciating pain and passed six other teams right at the finish line. We finished in second place. We had just earned the title and ranking as the second-best 4 x 800-meter relay team in the nation! My desire was specific and clear. No matter the pain and no matter the circumstance, I wanted to win. And so we did.

Desire requires action to back up the beliefs that you have. There are plenty of things to take action on, and we neglect most of them. But the fact that we have so many opportunities and options can always cause a conflict in our hearts. We need to eliminate the clutter and focus solely on what we want the most. During the relay race, I could've settled into the pack of runners and took maybe 10th or 11th place. But instead, I answered to my desire and did the unconventional and physically pushed through crowds of runners to gain what I obsessed over most. To me, desire is more than winning: it's obsessing.

Persistence

Persistence is desire's ultimate accelerator. In 2011, I reached the peak of my athletic performance. However, my cravings for athletics and not scholastics finally caught up with me. I lost all scholarships and Division I opportunities due to my poor A.C.T. scores and a grade average below embarrassing. Any scholarship opportunities I had once prospected were now no longer on the table.

I had two options: I could go back to school and raise my collegiate G.P.A. to compete at the collegiate level, or I could use the professional athlete loophole. This loophole allows an athlete who is not associated with a university to still compete in collegiate and amateur competitions as an unattached athlete. I desired to be the fastest and best athlete, and the quickest path to competing at the top was the option that still neglected my schooling and grades.

I put it all on the line and enrolled at the Colorado State Open Decathlon as an unattached athlete. It was a gamble, as it could ruin my track and field career and chances of landing a collegiate offer. But for me, it was all I desired: Do I earn my way onto a track team or compete like a pro on the road to Olympic dreams? The answer for me was a no-brainer.

Napoleon Hill said, "If you do not see great riches in your imagination, you will never see them in your bank balance." My burning desires have ultimately given me everything I have ever wanted and more. Every desire I achieve and obtain only opens my world up to more extraordinary, more desirable dreams that are worth pursuing.

My desires have led me to more than athletic performances. They've awarded me with many accolades, an amazing wife and family, a career as an award-winning international motivational speaker, and incredible friends and mentors like Erik "Mr. Awesome" Swanson, who've bestowed on me the opportunity of co-authoring in this series.

The Three Incontestable Attributes of Desire are a mere glimpse into the fulness of its power. I haven't stopped desiring and dreaming. I challenge everyone to seek and discover for themselves its eminence.

To find out what happened next in my desire to compete in the decathlon, you'll need to read our next book in this series.

JON KOVACH JR.

About Jon Kovach Jr.: Jon is an award-winning and international motivational speaker and global mastermind leader. Jon has helped multi-billion-dollar corporations, including Coldwell Banker Commercial, Outdoor Retailer Cotopaxi, and the Public Relations Student Society of America, exceed their annual sales goals. In his work as an accountability coach and mastermind facilitator, Jon has helped thousands of professionals overcome their challenges and achieve their goals by implementing his 4 Irrefutable Laws of High Performance.

Jon is Founder and Chairman of Champion Circle, a networking association that combines high-performance-based networking activities and recreational fun to create connection capital and increases prosperity for professionals.

Jon is the Mastermind Facilitator and Team Lead of the Habitude Warrior Mastermind and the Global Speakers Mastermind & Masterclass founded by Speaker Erik "Mr. Awesome" Swanson.

Jon speaks on a number of topics including Accountability, The 4 Irrefutable Laws of High Performance, and The Power of Mastermind Methodologies. Jon was recently featured in *SpeakUp TV*, an Amazon Prime TV series. He stars on over 75 speaking stages annually, podcasts and live shows as a host, emcee, and keynote speaker.

Author's website: *www.JonKovachJr.com*
Book Series Website & Author's Bio: *www.The13StepsToRiches.com*

Adora Evans

GAINING BACK WHAT YOU'VE LOST

I am eighteen years old, living in a boarded-up home with no electricity. I can see the brown walls because the drywall hasn't been added yet. I am eagerly fumbling with a cassette tape and a battery-operated Walkman radio.

A few days earlier a lady walked into the jewelry store where I worked and held up before and after pictures of her body showing she had lost over 100 pounds. She had lots of pictures of other people who lost weight, too. I had been wanting to lose weight, and she said if I bought this kit, I could lose weight and make money and she would teach me how.

So, instead of paying for my electricity, I bought the kit. It had the cassette tape I am pushing play on. It's by someone named Jim Rohn. I had a feeling that everything could change for me.

At this point in my life, I had already lived on my own and occasionally with friends. I was also the town scandal because I got married in high school to someone who was in college to be a preacher. I was our high school's Bible club president, and I was supposed to say a prayer at graduation. Instead, I ran away in the middle of the day with another guy, for no real reason that I could explain at the time.

So, while I once believed I was going to be a pastor's wife and used in ministry, I now believed that I had even failed God and that there was no real purpose for me.

Now, Jim Rohn is talking, and it seems like he is talking right to me. He is saying that we are all in a metaphorical sailboat, headed toward a destination that we will eventually arrive at. He says if we want to know where we are headed, we need to look at where we have been, the kinds of choices we have made, where our family members have ended up. It wasn't looking good for me. I started to feel down again, until he said something like, "Hey, if you don't believe in yourself, but you believe in me—believe in my belief in you." I did believe in him; he knew things I didn't know.

He said all you have to do is set your sail in a new direction. Then he said you need to get mentors. Who would mentor me? He continued, if you can't get a mentor, go to the library. There are all of these people who have put their life's wisdom into books, and you can read them for free.

I read seventy-five books that year and listened to I don't know how many audio programs. My life started to change. I earned a one-time check of almost nine thousand dollars.

Life was changing, and I could feel it, and others were beginning to see it. Later, I went on to work with celebrities, travel the world, and live many of my dreams. I wish I could tell you that it was all up from there, but it definitely wasn't. It was more like the stock market on the rise or a roller coaster with a consistent rise but with a lot of dips, drops, and mistakes. So, what does this story have to do with desire?

Well, in the middle of a dark room, in a small town, and at what felt like an emotional peak of loneliness, abandonment, helplessness, and shame, something else was also present. In the middle of very low self-esteem, and a feeling that I was no longer redeemable, because I felt I had screwed up, even with God—the most unconditional, loving being of them all. I felt I had ruined it. There was something beneath all that, fighting for me, and advocating for me, in spite of all of this. It felt like the tiniest spark of hope or belief, but little can become so much. That little thing was desire. The desire to change. The desire to have life be different for me. The desire to see that it could be different for my family and that maybe I wasn't all of these bad things that I believed about myself.

Desire is powerful, because it will often reveal itself to you, and it may not be something you are fully aware of at first. In fact, I think lots of people do not even know what they truly desire. Yes, I wanted more money, I wanted to be respected, I wanted to be a "good" person, but more than anything, I wanted to feel loved. I wanted to feel safe and to belong. I also wanted other things from having braces to living on beaches and even writing my own books—those were all self-expressions that made me feel some version of love, belonging, safety, and meaning.

Desire is the one thing that is always driving us all, either consciously or unconsciously. It may drive you to things you do not want. If you are subconsciously avoiding being abandoned and that desire is driving you, you may abandon others, choose unhealthy relationships, or avoid intimacy altogether. If you think the desire to be rich is driving you, but really the desire to be loved is driving you, and you think when you are rich enough you will be loved, you just may work too hard and sabotage and avoid the love relationships you have.

That is why it is very important to really spend the time getting to know yourself and your desires. You need to look at both the surface level of what you want next, whether it's a new outfit or a new business and then ask yourself, *Why do I want this? How is it going to make me feel?* Keep digging deeper—as deep as you can. When you hit the real desire, it will often make you cry, or feel a little silly or vulnerable, but this is magic, because when you know what you truly desire, then you can align your actions and your life consciously with what you are really wanting.

You will become absolutely unstoppable. When you don't know what you truly desire, you may find yourself spending equal energy working against yourself, so the growth will seem slow and hard. Remember: your deep desires are leading you, whether you like it or not, and whether you are aware of it or not. Doing the work of becoming aware of your desires allows you to leverage all of your energy more fully in the direction you actually want to go.

Many times, the desires you think you have were given to you by parents, celebrities, peers, or others. There are companies that spend millions of dollars working to capture your desire machine. They work to make you believe you will finally be loved, feel happy, or belong when you buy their purse, car, or belong to their club. Many have agendas for you, your money, and your time. That is why it is so important to take the agenda for you into your own hands.

Take the responsibility of knowing what makes you tick. What is moving you in life? What is the reason you do what you do? Why are you working in the field you are in? Why do you watch the shows you watch? Why do you have the friends you have? Why do you spend time with the people you spend time with? What desires are leading you?

This is the starting point for getting leverage on yourself and aligning with what is already happening inside of you and in your life. Then, you can begin to design the life you want and actually see your true desires come to light.

ADORA EVANS

About Adora Evans: Adora Evans is the author of the book Majestic Money: The 30-Day Femme Manifesting Game. Adora has led hundreds of thousands of women around the world to tap into their feminine power to create more money, love, and miracles in their lives. As a womb healer, she leads women on a sacred journey of self-love and personal discovery as they learn to heal the blocks holding them back from their inner brilliance and sacred abundance. Adora is a magnetic, loving power, goddess, and mystic. As a seasoned entrepreneur and founder of Body Legacy, Adora went from a boarded-up home with no electricity at 18 years old to working with celebrities on red carpets. Adora Evans has been facilitating this transformational work for 20 years as a coach, healer, teacher, and spiritual guide.

Author's website: *www.AdoraCrystal.com*
Book Series Website & Author's Bio: *www.The13StepsToRiches.com*

DESIRE TO LIVE A DREAM LIFE

When I was a kid, I desired to help people and live a dream life. I came to America from Mexico at 11 years old, lived in the projects, and worked in the fields. I read *Reader's Digest* and learned empowering success stories; I made them part of me and my life.

At age 13, I worked at a grocery store, and they put me in charge. At 16, I got a job in a manufacturing company while still going to high school. Because of my hard work, at 17, I was the only kid with a brand-new car. I got paid every Friday, and I would invite all my friends for lunch. I dressed well and lived well.

I became a father at a very young age, at 18. When I saw that little boy, I promised him that I would work three jobs if it meant he would always be okay. I did exceptionally well. I got a career in the aerospace industry, and at that time, there were no Latinos in management. I was the first one, and not only was I Latino, but I was a young Latino. Immediately, I started going up the ranks and got into management in my early 20s. I started traveling for Rockwell International, traveling to different military bases to train personnel. I was living a great life.

Then, one day, I got more intense about my burning desires after a friend of mine lent me a book called *Common Sense,* by Al Williams. It referenced *Think and Grow Rich,* by Napoleon Hill. I started studying the book, devouring it, and then I concluded that I wasn't born to have a job or have a career. I was born to be an entrepreneur and to live a dream life.

I knew what I wanted to do, so I got into finance. I started doing loans. I did that for about six months before I got into real estate. In my first year in the business, I closed over 80 deals, which was unheard of at the time. I did all of this with that passion and burning desire to help people and empower them to live a dream life. I became a manager in a company with only nine people, and in three years, I grew that company to almost 100 agents.

One day, the company owner was a little rude to me, and I told them, "I don't want a job. I want a career, something that I can manage, something that I can have a little bit more control over."

With my experience in real estate, I was very familiar with government contracts. The nearby Air Force base was closing, and we were able to get 570 listings in the inland empire and 370 listings up in northern California using my expertise. In Vallejo, we did really, really well. We were in five locations and had about 300 agents. That's where I learned how to see the bigger picture.

One major habitude (habit and attitude) in developing a burning desire that I've learned is doing the right thing, even when it's hard, and then doing it with a burning passion. Your happiness and fulfillment will strengthen your integrity.

We were doing well, but then my business partner brought a family member into management. I disagreed with her philosophy, so I said, "No problem, I'm just going to keep this office, and I gave him the four other offices." I gave up much of our hard-earned money and work because of the disagreement; however, I opened up the most significant Century 21 office in the Inland Empire shortly after. Again, I had a burning desire to help others and live a dream life. Following this formula, I felt unstoppable.

Things were going great until 2010, when I went through a divorce. Despite this emotional tragedy, I still had that burning desire to do something big. And because of the people I know, there were many distress sales at the local, state, and federal levels. I talked with a group at the five banks called National Asian American Coalition. I took money out of my pocket and joined that organization.

There are many defense mechanisms in this world. Many people choose to play dead when the going gets tough. If you play through, which some animals do when being attacked, you become a victim. Like a leaf from a tree, you're going to wither away if you don't take a proactive approach and allow that burning desire to feel your passion and ambition go out and do things that are bigger than you.

With the help of friends and strategic partnerships, we've been able to manage even the Great Recession of 2008, including Eric Swanson, who has been very instrumental in helping us grow and promote our live-hour show, *Boost for The Day*. He and others have empowered many people on the front, through teaching and coaching, by sharing that example of a burning desire.

Be Principle-Oriented

How do you work when you don't feel like working? How do you work when your passion is not a vision?

The scriptures say, "for we walk by faith, not by sight," and if faith is lacking in our vision and passion, our burning desires become our circumstances. Things do turn out the way you want them to. With that said, honor and amplify your wants.

Most people acknowledge that life has no handouts, and everything happens to you. Develop a mindset that it doesn't happen *to* you, but it happens *for* you. You also need the stamina and energy to continue forward.

Do you want to play dead, or do you want to play? Do you want to play not to lose, or do you want to play to win?

One thing that I teach our people about developing their burning desires is focusing your mindset away from being competitive. I tell them competing with others is being average. To win, you've got to be dominant in the game. When Michael Jordan and Kobe Bryant walk onto the court, they play to win. They don't play to compete. Not only do they win, but they also dominate the game. If you don't have that burning desire and level of passion, maybe you should get a job.

Techniques and Strategies

You can lead a horse to water, but you can't make them drink.

My dad grew up on a farm. He used to say, "That's because you don't know horses... you take the horse's mouth to whatever it looks like the water, and you're going to create a thirst in its life." When you're working with people and serving people, you always have to create that thirst, that hunger, in them by leading their mouths closer to what looks like water.

I have found that any time that I'm indecisive or double-minded, I am reminded that somebody who is a double-minded person is unstable in all his ways. You can deal with indecision emotionally, or you can flip a coin. When you flip a coin, it's tough to take the possibility of landing somewhere more disappointing. I flip, but I throw the coin. If I don't feel good, I call tails knowing it is the right choice. If it feels good, I call it heads confident it is the right choice; your intuition is calling, and you need to listen to it.

When it comes to up-leveling yourself, my final advice and counsel is to never look down on anyone, unless that person has fallen and you're going to help them. My way always works from a servant attitude.

When seeking your burning desires, stop telling people, and start asking them. I always operate from a position of influence and now from a place of power, and you will grasp more and do more and be more influential and powerful in a shorter time. I was nominated to be the president of a board of realtors.

AMADO HERNANDEZ

About Amado Hernandez: With 33 years of Real Estate experience, Mr. ABC Amado Hernandez successfully continues to operate and grow his Excellence Empire Real Estate Moreno Valley office. Broker/Owner Amado first opened his doors in 1995 and Excellence currently has over 60 offices in Southern California, Las Vegas, and Merida Yucatan Mexico and over 900 Agents. He is also part owner of a highly successful Mortgage company Excellence Mortgage and owner of Empire Escrow Services. Mr. Amado is also involved with his community and currently serves as Director at Inland Valley Association of Realtors and will be the President Elect for 2021.

Always enthusiastic for life and eager to learn, Amado transformed himself from engineer to entrepreneur. "Having a job was okay, but being an entrepreneur was better." He is constantly in search of quality Agents who will have the benefit of his one-on-one coaching, leadership, and expertise. I am looking for "Executive Chefs, not order taker".

Author's website: *www.ExcellenceEmpireRE.com*
Book Series Website & Author's Bio: *www.The13StepsToRiches.com*

Angelika Ullsperger

WHAT IS DESIRE?

Desire is where everything starts. All of the changes made in the world happened because someone desired it. They desired it so much they did anything to bring their ideas to fruition.

Desire is where it all begins. It starts with a tiny thought coincidentally slipping in your head. It fumbles around in the back of your mind and begins to set in. Over time the desire brews inside of you, creating a feeling so strong you know without a doubt nothing will stop you. A desire so strong it makes you almost invincible.

Desire is the seed you plant at the beginning of your journey, your thoughts and actions will be the sun and rain that fuel your growth. You must make sure it receives proper sun and rain so it can prosper. With bad weather or no care at all, the plant is helpless and will die. If you do not contribute to your goals, you will begin to lose your desire and grow to be weak in passion. But just as the plant with proper care, your ideas can grow strong and create something beautiful.

Every day you have a choice to get up and work towards anything in the world that you want. And every day you do nothing, your desire slips away whether you know it or not. When you tune in to those desires, that is when the magic begins.

My first run-in with true desire was through a guy named Mannie. I couldn't tell you how we met, but I can tell you that my life wouldn't be where it is now if it wasn't for him. When I met him, I could tell something about him was very different. But what was it? What was so different about him?

It was his desire for riches.

Never before had I met anyone who developed a burning desire so strong that it emanated through his entire being.

I could feel his determination for success just by being near him. He desired success so strongly, he was pulled to work his hardest every single day. He was so passionate he never took a day off. That was the first time I had ever met someone who cultivated such strong desire.

 Seeing how determined he was to get what he desired started to stir the desire within me. His presence in my life showed me the strength of a true burning desire and inspired me to delve further into the world of richness.

I was always very driven but was constantly ending up in traumatic situations. At one point in time, I had ended up in an abusive relationship with a sociopath. It broke me but I healed.

Soon after though my mom's partner of four years was shot and killed on our property. Subsequently, things got so bad the only way I could escape into safety was in my dreams. I slept almost every hour of the day, only getting up occasionally to eat or waste time scrolling through my phone. I didn't want to live this way.

There comes a point when it's no longer living, it's surviving. It wasn't a way to live. Many times the thought of suicide crossed my mind. There was nothing left inside me, my mind was filled with meaningless static. No thoughts, just an empty shell, going through days, months, years. Sometimes not even doing the bare minimum to function.

The emotional pain was so strong that physical pain began to envelop my body. My heart stung with pain, the only thing left in my near lifeless body. So many times, more than I will ever remember, I wanted to give up for good and end it.

But something was stopping me.

Desire.

A small fire still burned in the ashes of the person I used to be, a fire that kept pulling me forward. Even when every ounce of my being wanted to give up, the desire prevailed. In all of the pain I went through, I found solace in helping others when I couldn't help myself.

After knowing the true extent of pain, I didn't want anyone else to continue living in such a state. There was a desire to help. A desire to show the world regardless of what you go through, who you are, or where you come from, success *is* possible. And it all starts with cultivating your desire.

In the beginning, my desire was weak but like many skills, desire can be worked like a muscle. It can be strengthened by doing the proper exercises. Just as you can get stronger physically, you can get stronger mentally. This stands true regardless of how bad your mental health is. And just like a muscle, if you don't use it, the strength begins to fade away whether or not you notice. So use it!

So, how can you mold your desires into a burning passion?

By spending time with your dreams.

One of the best ways is through visualization. Close your eyes, take a deep breath and visualize the future you want. Visualize having already hit that goal. How does that make you feel? What is the next step you can take to get there? Not the next ten steps, one at a time. This keeps you from getting overwhelmed, because when you get overwhelmed you stop taking action. Therefore it's important to make sure you're not trying to do everything all at once by yourself. It's a journey, not a race. Take it day by day, and as long as you never give up, you will get there.

Starting your day off right happens the night before. Fall asleep as you visualize your dreams and desires. When you awake, recount your desires. Write them down three times a day to keep them at the front of your conscious mind. And if anyone ever says your dreams are too big, get rid of them and get even bigger dreams. It's going to be pertinent that you remove all negativity in your life and replace it with positivity.

Find others who have similar desires, people who inspire you to grow. Share your dreams with them. Use the power of the group to help fuel your desire for greatness.

Surround yourself with reminders of your goals. Begin to saturate your mind with thoughts of your desires until you develop a burning obsession. Become so obsessed that you no longer have to push yourself. You will have a burning obsession to pull you forward.

Sometimes your desires won't be achieved quickly. Sometimes it will take a lot of time, but that is where the difference between the successful and unsuccessful lies. Successful people know if they keep working at it, if they keep going they *will* make it. There are no if, ands, or buts. They carve their desire into a definite reality, because the desire is so strong they are willing to do anything to get there. They change success from just a possibility to a reality. Create a reality in which success is the only option.

Once you become filled with desire, you will be filled with the motivation to do anything to get there. A strong desire will create a massive resilience within your heart. When these strengths combine you become infallible. Regardless of what hurdles and hardships you face, and regardless of if you fail, your desire and resilience will pull you back up. Everyone will "fail" in life but you can choose to use the pull of desire to turn this "failure" into a lesson to keep you growing.

As long as you are taking action, your goal can be in your future, but the second you stop and give up, all possibilities of that goal that once made you ready and willing to move mountains, vanish.

That is the beauty and strength of desire, use it correctly and it will pull you towards your dreams. True failure only occurs when you lose your desire and stop moving towards a goal. Just as your desire to live can be the difference between life or death, your desire to bring your dreams to fruition will be the difference between true success and true failure.

Whatever you get from reading this chapter, use that energy to keep up your momentum. Take that desire and take instant action to get closer to achieving your goals.

ANGELIKA ULLSPERGER

About Angelika Ullsperger: Angelika is a polymorph entrepreneur from Baltimore, Maryland. Not only is she a fashion designer, model, artist, and musician, she also works as a business owner, a carpenter, and a coach. She has plenty of tricks up her sleeve but her main job is to do whatever she can to help others and make a positive impact. Filled with resilience from her past traumas of abuse and witnessing the murder of someone very special to her, she is determined to prove to the world regardless of who you are or where you come from you can make success happen.

Author's website: *www.Angelika.world*
Book Series Website & Author's Bio: *www.The13StepsToRiches.com*

DEFINING DESIRE

Think and Grow Rich by Napoleon Hill is one of the best classic books to teach someone about how to become a financial success (as well as a success in other areas of life). Within it, you will find thirteen steps to riches; each one has its own separate chapter and analysis. The subject of our book is to interpret his first step to riches: desire. Desire is extremely important and should be at the top of the list, above all other steps mentioned in Hill's work. However, as I will show, the first step to riches should begin with "purpose." But first, let's start with an understanding of the concept of desire.

What is desire? Although Hill never clearly defines "desire" in Chapter 2, he alludes to his meaning many times. For example, he did not mean it to be a *hope* or a *wish*, but something more *definite*. He says, "But *desiring* riches with a state of mind that becomes an obsession, then planning definite ways and means to acquire riches, and backing those plans with persistence which *does not recognize failure*, will bring riches" (Hill, 2011, p. 56). Contrarily, Merriam-Webster dictionary defines desire as 1) (verb) to long or hope for: exhibit or feel desire for; 2) (verb) to express a wish for; or 3) (noun) impulse toward something that promises enjoyment or satisfaction in its attainment.

Hill also gave two major examples in his second chapter of people who used desire to become rich: Edwin C. Barnes and Blair Hill (Napoleon's son). First, Edwin C. Barnes became successful, despite his handicaps of being poor and without any connections of influence. He achieved his goal of working with the inventor Thomas Edison because of his burning desire to do so and implementation of his plan. On the other hand, Blair Hill was born physically handicapped without any signs of ears. Despite this, Blair's burning desire to hear led him to find a solution and then to later become a spokesman for the deaf. Although both of these individuals also possessed many other traits discussed in *Think and Grow Rich*, having a burning desire was the characteristic which sparked all others.

In short, I think that Hill's version of desire means to want something so much that everything in your life revolves around achieving your goal. Alternatively, desire can be viewed as the word "want" on steroids. If you compare this definition to Merriam-Webster's above, you will notice that they are still very similar.

Desire can also be likened to an extreme version of a wish or hope (even though Hill states otherwise). If you desire something, you will do whatever it takes to ensure that you get it. All of your thoughts will be laser-focused on the actions required to meet your goal. These are the traits that Edwin, Blair, and other successful people have, that is, the ability to want and act on their desired goal. Desire can be compared to the fuel in a car. The fuller your tank, the further you will go. If you have a full tank of desire, you have a better chance of achieving your goals.

Hill's desire can also be used in the context of life, as well as financial success. At the end of the chapter, he gives an example of a business associate that survived only because of "his own desire to live" (Hill, 2011, p. 77). Using my definition above, this man had wanted to live so badly that every aspect of his life became obsessed with achieving his goal. What is being called a "desire to live" can be equivalent to what is commonly titled the "will to live." In my *The Survival of the Richest* book, I had a similar conclusion: "I do agree that a person must not only be *able* to survive, but must *want* to as well. This desire is a common theme found in survival books. It is represented by a phrase that every survival expert knows, although few attempt to define it: 'the will to live'"(Criniti, 2016, p. 12).

I also interpret the word "desire" to offer a choice. If you desire something, you are choosing to want it. This is the reason that the word "desirable" was inserted into the goal of survival: "The major goal of survival and survivalism is for a living entity to stay alive for the maximum desirable amount of time" (Criniti, 2016, p. 16). Only if you desire to live longer than your normal life expectancy will you have the most use for studying the science of survival. But this will depend on how long you *choose* to stay alive.

It is important to now discuss why the first step to riches should not be desire, but instead, purpose. Although Hill is using his term in regards to becoming mostly a financial success, our clues can again be found through studying survival. "Reflect on this: Why would anyone desire to live, if he can't find at least one reason? The difficulty you may have in answering this tough question is why I ranked having a purpose to live higher than a will to live. *Simply, someone who wants to live must have a reason for it, regardless of what it is. In contrast, someone with a reason to live might still not want to live.* Maybe the reason is just not good enough!" (Criniti, 2016, p. 115). For example, someone who commits suicide might have had many good reasons to live but still wanted to die. But everyone who desires to live must have some underlying reason to want to stay alive (for example, to be with their family).

The logic for always ranking a purpose as a higher priority over a desire to live (a.k.a. "will to live") is also applicable to anything else that you desire, especially financial success. If you desire to grow exponentially rich, there still must be a reason. What is your purpose for wanting to be rich in the first place? This is why I think Napoleon's analysis should have first started with purpose as the first step to grow riches. I am not discounting the role of desire, not one bit actually. I am simply stating that the real foundation to building a house of wealth needs to first start with the answer to the question, "Why?"

Finally, although a purpose should always come before desire, it should be unquestionably clear that having both a purpose and a desire should come before everything else. From the context of survival, this is especially true and became a major conclusion of my last book: "Thus, obtaining any of the survival essentials is irrelevant if a person doesn't have a reason or the will to live. These two items are unquestionably the most important survival essentials" (Criniti, 2016, p. 116). Learning about the science of survival is useless if someone doesn't have a purpose or a desire to live. Similarly, learning about any of Hill's laws of success, his steps to riches, or finance in general is useless if one does not have a reason or a desire to do it. In short, you need *meaning* to spark your *desire*; and you need *desire* to make your successes *meaningful.*

In conclusion, Napoleon Hill's first step to riches should have been *purpose*, instead of *desire*; however, it is forgivable, because his analysis and examples clearly demonstrate the priority of desire over all of the other steps to riches in *Think and Grow Rich*. It is also important to note why we should desire to be rich in the first place. From my *The Necessity of Finance* book: "Every individual, group, or organization needs money to live and desires more money rather than less; consequentially, they also desire more wealth, as money is just a part of wealth. If they don't focus on increasing their money and their overall wealth, the alternative is to survive poorly" (Criniti, 2013, p. 20). In short, desire should be used as one of your best financial weapons to not only "grow rich," but to simultaneously ensure that you survive and prosper.

Bibliography

Criniti, Anthony M., IV. 2013. *The Necessity of Finance: An Overview of the Science of Management of Wealth for an Individual, a Group, or an Organization*. Philadelphia: Criniti Publishing.

Criniti, Anthony M., IV. 2016. *The Survival of the Richest: An Analysis of the Relationship between the Sciences of Biology, Economics, Finance, and Survivalism*. Philadelphia: Criniti Publishing.

Hill, Napoleon. 2011. *Think and Grow Rich*. United Kingdom: Capstone Publishing Ltd.

Merriam-Webster: https://www.merriam-webster.com/dictionary/desire

DR. ANTHONY M. CRINITI IV

About Dr. Anthony M. Criniti IV: Dr. Anthony (aka "Dr. Finance") is the world's leading financial scientist and survivalist. A fifth generation native of Philadelphia, Dr. Criniti is a former finance professor at several universities, a former financial planner, an active investor in diverse marketplaces, an explorer, an international keynote speaker, and has traveled around the world studying various aspects of finance. He is an award winning author of three #1 international best-selling finance books: The Necessity of Finance (2013), The Most Important Lessons in Economics and Finance (2014), and The Survival of the Richest (2016). As a prolific writer, he also frequently contributes articles to Entrepreneur, Medium, and Thrive Global. Dr. Criniti's work has started a grassroots movement that is changing the way that we think about economics and finance.

Author's website: *www.DrFinance.info*
Book Series Website & Author's Bio: *www.The13StepsToRiches.com*

Barry Bevier

ON DESIRE

I spent over thirty years in an engineering career where perfection was essential. We designed foundations for bridges, buildings, evaluated the safety of dams, repaired landslides, and stabilized eroding coastlines. Even a slight error could mean a very expensive repair, a collapse, or even death. We had to be perfect. As a result, I overthink things a lot in most aspects of my life. So when I jumped on the opportunity to participate in this book project, the first thing I did was go to Webster's and see how the dictionary defines desire.

Merriam Webster's online dictionary defines desire as "conscious impulse towards something that promises enjoyment or satisfaction in its attainment." I also googled desire and found that psychologists subdivide desire into sixteen different categories: power, independence, curiosity, acceptance, order, saving, honor, idealism, social contact, family status, vengeance, romance, eating, physical exercise, and tranquility. Wow, who would have thought!

So, as I thought back on my life, and how desire has come into play in bringing me to where I am in my life today, I have to say that until the past few years, it really didn't. I was raised on a midwest farm, in a mid-twentieth century Protestant culture where we were taught to fear God and be thankful and content with what He had provided us. Desiring to have more was considered greedy and sinful. I remember my mother saying that it was God's will for Christians and farmers to be poor and that wealthy people are evil and will take advantage of others.

As a result, I was never taught, or given examples of dreaming, of setting goals, of planning for a future that I could only imagine in my youth. To me, it seemed Christian philosophy and tradition took a dim view of the desire to have the earthly satisfactions of this world rather than the eternal rewards of Heaven.

I've since learned that most western philosophers, on the other hand, generally view desire as fundamental to human life—to be human is to desire what we do not have.

So with that Christian philosophy embedded in my subconscious at a young age, how did I end up having a pretty successful, satisfying life?

As I think back to when I was growing up, there were a lot of things that I did desire and worked hard to attain. Although at that point in time, I really didn't consider them desires.

Growing up near Detroit and having many family members involved in the auto industry, I became passionate about cars. One of my uncles was involved with Ford's corporate NASCAR racing team and had a collection of two seater Thunderbirds.

As a young teen, I became very interested in T-Birds and decided that on my sixteenth birthday, I would own one. For at least three years, I worked in any way I could: working on my dad's farm, mowing neighbor's lawns, clearing snow in the wintertime, helping other farmers with their planting and harvests, repairing cars. By the time I was sixteen, I had earned and saved enough money to buy my first car—a '57 Thunderbird (which I still own today).

So that was a desire that I didn't realize as such at the time. While I enjoyed the work I was doing for others, it was merely a vehicle to raise the money to be able to buy the car when I turned sixteen and was able to drive it.

When I was in high school, getting an engineering degree, having an engineering career, and owning my own engineering company was never a dream or desire. It somehow materialized by being passionate about the work it took to get there. I love math and science. I studied hard to get good grades, driven by the desire to learn as much as I could, not so much for the grades, and not really so much to get accepted at a great university. It was simply to gain as much knowledge as I could.

Likewise, in college, as I was completing my senior year and graduate years, I had no idea where my education would take me. Yet opportunities came up which I took advantage of, often with little or no hesitation. It all resulted in a great career.

So when I look at it, my success was not a result of a desire at the core. It was a result of being passionate about the work and activities it took to reach the achievement. It didn't start with a dream and a desire to achieve that dream.

After my wife passed away a few years ago, I became exposed to personal development for the first time through network marketing. One of my first experiences was with Jim Rohn and Zig Ziglar and the concept of dreaming and setting goals and planning. By being strategic with daily activities, having a plan and consistently always moving toward it (even if it is slow), one can achieve those goals and realize the dream.

I think the first thing that I consciously did desire and really went for was when I met Linda. I did have a strong desire to be with her the rest of my life. And fortunately, it was mutual, and we were able to spend twelve wonderful years together.

One of my favorite sayings has become, "You don't know what you don't know." Not too long after Linda passed away, I recognized that, even though we thought we were living a healthy lifestyle (and we probably were compared to the majority of the population) there were lifestyle changes we could have made that would have helped her health.

Coupled with the exposure to personal development through network marketing, I realized that I had a new strong desire. I realized that I was developing a strong desire to leave my engineering career and find a way to help people avoid what happened to our family.

I had a burning desire to learn as much as I could about natural wellness, about how people could get healthy and stay healthy without the aid of pharmaceuticals. I learned about taking our health into our own hands and making day-to-day decisions that can improve our health and wellbeing. There was a financial cost to this, which I have been willing to pay to achieve the outcome.

Because the desire to help others avoid the pain and grief that our family did after her passing was so strong, I have taken a new path.

It's taken several years, but that desire is finally coming to fruition for me, becoming affiliated with Stemtech, the first company to develop nutritional supplements that release your own stem cells and becoming a Certified Brain Health Coach through Amen Clinics.

I've also learned that desire, burning desire, is the first step in manifesting what we would like to see happen in our lives. And through this process I've been able to build the self confidence that I can do anything I desire and put my mind to. Henry Ford had a saying: "Whether you think you can or think you can't, you're right." And I'm ridding my subconscious of the archaic views instilled in me as a youth about wealth.

My desire is to help people with their health and wellness, as well as in other ways.

I also have another new desire, building homes for less-fortunate people in third world countries. Growing up on a farm, I learned to do almost everything mechanical and in construction. My engineering career afforded me the opportunity to travel and work internationally, which I quickly learned to love. With the desire to help others, this combination of skills and experience brought a new idea to the surface. I make a trip each year to Belize to help build housing for poor families through a local church.

Without me being financially fit, I would not be able to take these trips and bless others with the talents God has blessed me with. I remember hearing Jim Rohn say, "Money isn't everything, but it's right up there with oxygen."

I am so glad to have cleared all those limiting beliefs from my youth out of my head and am now free to follow my desires and to impact others in a meaningful way.

BARRY BEVIER

About Barry Bevier: Barry Bevier is a proud father of two amazing daughters in their mid-twenties, who are pursuing their passions in psychology and architecture in Southern California. He was raised on a family farm near Ann Arbor, Michigan. Growing up, he developed his faith in God, a strong work ethic, a love for nature, and a passion to help others. After completing his master's degree in civil engineering at the University of Michigan, he pursued a career in engineering, which eventually brought him to Southern California.

In 2000, he married the love of his life, Linda. They shared a beautiful life for ten years, until she succumbed to the effects of lupus and 20 years of treatment with prescription medications. Since then, Barry pivoted his career path into educating and helping others. By has educated himself in alternative, natural modalities in wellness and became a Licensed Brain Health Trainer through Amen Clinic.. He also works with a new technology in stem cell supplementation that releases your own stem cells.

Author's website: *www.BrBevier.stemtech.com*
Book Series Website & Author's Bio: *www.The13StepsToRiches.com*

SERVING OTHERS

What is desire? Is it something we're born with? How does it work? I know I had an innate desire to be a part of this world and to make an impact. It wasn't until years later that I learned my desire had the power to profoundly impact others.

I am sitting in my home office, plastered with the paintings my two kids, my Monkeys, have made over the years. My daughter, a senior in high school, walked into the room, and sat down in the chair next to me.

"Here, Dad, read this speech I wrote for a contest at school." She held out a few pieces of paper. I assumed she wanted to run it past me before presenting before an audience.

I began to read aloud, "Speech Contest Essay: Live To Inspire. This story, about to be told, is about an extraordinary man, now forty-two years young, who has accepted all the obstacles life had thrown at him. Now I know you may be thinking that everyone has different obstacles they just overcome throughout their lifetime, so how is he different from you and I? What makes this particular man different from you and I is the tactics he used when faced with these obstacles. What makes him different from you and

I is that he took these obstacles and used them to help make a difference and inspire others to never let life get in the way of their greatness and achievements. What makes any one of us different from everyone else is not the obstacles life throws at us, but what we do when faced with these obstacles. Will you choose to accept defeat or choose to persevere?"

On May 13, 1975, a child was born at Cedars-Sinai Medical Center in Los Angeles, CA. This child was born three months prematurely, weighing 1 1/2 pounds.

During the 1980s, he was diagnosed with a neurological disorder called Tourette Syndrome, which is a type of tic disorder characterized by involuntary, repetitive movements and vocalization. He went to various doctors who performed countless medical examinations to try and find a cure. Every doctor said the same thing: He's fine, he will grow out of it.

One day in fifth grade he stood up in front of his entire class and shared with them what Tourette Syndrome was and what living with Tourette Syndrome was like. A huge weight was lifted off of his shoulders once he shared his story with his classmates and it generated many supporters among friends, parents, and teachers.

Finally a specialist at UCLA told him that he would never be able to get rid of this disorder alone and suggested that he take a special drug called Clonidine to help with the tics. Unfortunately, with this drug came horrible side effects. He made a conscious decision to not take the pills after a few years and try to master his condition through focus and determination. After a while, the tics started to diminish and for the most part went away.

No one knows what life has in store for them. All we can do is live until we are forced to face an obstacle in which we must make a choice to overcome or accept defeat.

With the experiences this boy had to face, came a life lesson: With determination, perseverance, and support from others anything can happen.

Now, at forty-two years young, this man chooses to use his story to make a difference in others' lives by inspiring people in times of uncertainty. He implements the Rotary's motto, 'Service Before Self,' by finding the light in those who cannot find it in themselves, and supporting them through their tough obstacles. He helps lift people's spirits and hopes in times of hopelessness and despair. He helps people turn their ideas and dreams into realities. He helps build people from the ground up in hopes that they too will one day share their stories with others. He makes a difference in the world each and every day, which inspires others to make a difference as well.

Who may you ask, is this man? Well, he is my father. Out of all the lives' he has made the biggest difference in, I believe he has made the biggest difference in mine. He inspires me never to give up on what I believe in, to always do what makes me happy but most importantly, to always live every day as if it were the last, because we are never guaranteed a tomorrow. As Gandhi once said, 'Be the change you wish to see in the world.' Making a difference in the lives of others is my dad's change. What will be yours?

To say I was completely taken aback is an understatement. Before that moment, I had no idea that she felt that way about me. It brought me to tears. In that moment, we hugged and cried together as my heart smiled with the pride of being her father.

I chose to tell you my story through my daughter's heart, because often we're blind to how our personal desire positively impacts those around us.

I'm frequently asked, "How can you be so happy and positive all the time given what you've experienced? How do you do it?"

The answer: Desire. The desire to be a source of positivity in the world for others.

The first time I experienced this desire was in high school. Even today, I remember the moment. I was passing a classmate on the stairs in a crowd of kids, when out of the corner of my eye, I saw three tics one right after the other and knew instantly he had Tourette's. I knew then I wasn't alone, and wanted him to know he wasn't alone.

We had a moment; a moment that would change both of our lives forever. He had no idea "what was wrong with himself," and neither did his parents.

That day, I found a super-power I never knew I had. A gift. My voice. I went home to my Mom, told her I knew my classmate had Tourette's, and asked, "What can we do to help?"

Our families met, and after a lengthy conversation and time together, we wound up leading them to the same doctor that diagnosed me at UCLA Medical Center.

Growing up as the small, weird kid I dealt with adversity and bullying, daily. I would come home to my mom crying because I didn't understand why people were being mean to me. Why couldn't I be like everyone else? I just wanted to blend in.

I couldn't stand the thought of another child crying on the floor with their dog, holding him and knowing he was his only friend. Through helping my classmate, my desire to help others became my mission. I knew that I could be a giver of good, positivity, love, strength, encouragement and that I would shine my light on others.

I know every breath I take is a gift. I have failed more than I have succeeded. I know I could focus on the negative. Desire is why I have succeeded, regardless of the outcome. With a purpose to be the good in the universe, no matter how bad my day was, no matter what happened to me, I would "give out good" 365 days a year with the intention to achieve my Why; to inspire one person a day.

With desire leading my purpose, I know that at the end of each day, I have achieved my Why, if I have inspired one person to chase after their dreams (their desire) and empowered them so that they know, feel and believe they are capable of accomplishing anything!

My goal is that everyone is motivated to get up one more time after they've fallen 50,000 times, and to believe in themselves, knowing they can get back up, go again and that they are succeeding every time they do, regardless of achieving their goal. In inspiring one person to inspire someone else, I have accomplished my Why. When I put a smile on a person's face, or make one person feel good about themselves, my desire has prevailed!

When I accomplish even one of these things each day, I have fulfilled my desire of, and have done my part as a human being toward, making the world a better place.

Life has thrown curveballs at me. I'll keep getting up to the plate and swinging, because my mom's in my head reminding me, "You fought for every breath to make it into this world. You're a fighter."

The excitement I felt when a friend wanted to play with me, came from feeling accepted. I work hard to make sure others feel included, wanted, loved, and valued; not judged, but truly appreciated for their authentic-self.

You are not alone. We are here to support one another. We are better and stronger together.

Life has thrown curveballs at me. I'll keep getting up to the plate and swinging, because my mom's in my head reminding me, "You fought for every breath to make it into this world. You're a fighter."

My desire is to inspire everyone, to believe that you have a voice, a story, and that you matter. Have the confidence that your voice and story will positively impact and inspire another human being's life. It took me many years to learn this truth.

There is no greater gift to give or receive.

In doing this, I feel I have gifted people the "power of desire."

BRIAN SCHULMAN

About Brian Schulman: Brian is known as the Godfather and Pioneer of LinkedIn Video and one of the world's premiere live streaming and video marketing experts. He has 20+ years of proven Digital Marketing experience strategizing with IR500 & Fortune500 brands across the globe. An internationally known Keynote Speaker, Brian founded and is the CEO of Voice Your Vibe, which brings his wealth of knowledge as an advisor and mentor to Founders and C-Suite Executives by providing workshops and one-on-one Mastery Coaching on how to voice their vibe, attract their tribe, and tell a story that people will fall in love with through the power and impact of live and pre-recorded video. Named "2020 Best LIVE Festive Show of The Year" at the IBM TV Awards, his weekly LIVE shows #ShoutOutSaturday and #WhatsGoodWednesday have aired live for more than 300 consecutive episodes and have been featured in Forbes, Thrive Global, Yahoo Finance, an Amazon best-selling book and syndicated on a Smart TV Network. Among his many awards and honors, Brian has been named a "LinkedIn Top Voice," "LinkedIn Video Creator Of The Year," one of the "Top 50 Most Impactful People of LinkedIn," and a "LinkedIn Global Leader of The Year" for two consecutive years.

Author's website: *www.VoiceYourVibe.com*
Book Series Website & Author's Bio: *www.The13StepsToRiches.com*

Bryce McKinley

LISTENING TO THE SIGNS

The fight or flight response is an automatic physiological reaction to an event perceived as stressful or frightening. The perception of threat activates the sympathetic nervous system and triggers an acute stress response that prepares the body to fight or flee.

For me, desire means when you face immense pressure and encounter the option to "fight or flight," you choose to fight!

I remember the moment vividly. The night was hot; my emotions were raw and ragged. I sat in the front seat of the car that had become my home, with my infant son sleeping in his car seat behind me, the gun I had pointed in my mouth jammed! It had never done that before, nor has it since, but that night, not once, not twice, but three times.

I had just gotten off the phone with my brother, discussing a new business idea. On a high note, we were both feeling good. But within twenty minutes of hanging up, my mindset shifted back to my current and desperate reality; homeless and in a brutal custody battle with my son's biological mother. Months of court battles and lawyer fees had burned through my savings and sunk me deep into feelings of giving up.

My world was crumbling, and everything felt too challenging to overcome. With only thirty-two dollars left to my name, I used a tattered piece of paper to write a tearful letter to my son. Then, I pulled out onto a busy street, knowing that somebody would find my son and find his mother's contact information in my letter. Like a robot on autopilot, I pulled the slide to cock the gun, put it in my mouth, and as I pulled the trigger, it jammed.

A lot happens at that moment; memories, priorities, purpose, regrets, anger, sorrow, and the fragmented feelings of God all come rushing. With my life flashing before me, I instantly remembered growing up in a rigorous and cult-like religion. When I was eleven, my parents separated, and my mom moved into low-income housing. Like every kid my age in the area, I got involved in gangs, drugs, and violence.

Between eleven and seventeen, I fathered a beautiful daughter yet got arrested and put in handcuffs more times than I can count.

Unimpressed with my lifestyle, my uncle, a businessman, immediately changed my unfavorable habits by putting me to work, sleeping on his couch, and instituting strict rules with curfews.

He taught me how to show care and attention to myself and my potential by detailing cars at his car dealership. There, working alongside him, I fell in love with the automotive industry. I saw how the cars created value, how the salesmen offered a service, and the customers bought what they wanted.

A few months later, in the middle of a blizzard, none of the other salesmen showed up for work. There was no action at the dealership, and that's when my uncle said, "If you can sell a car today, I'll put you on the sales team."

It was my chance to shift my life. That day, with only guts and gumption, I sold three cars! The next day, I went through the phone book, cold-called people, reached out to those scheduled to come in for oil changes, and got them to book a sales appointment with me. That sales call converted them into buyers.

That is when I learned a powerful life-changing lesson of sales; selling is a service. With that new entrepreneurial mindset, I became unstoppable.

In just two and a half years, I became the number one car salesman in the world! Yes, the world! Ford Motor Company™ recruited me out of my dealership with a multi-million-dollar deal and had me traveling to struggling dealerships and new dealerships where I implemented what is now known today as the 5-Star Blue Oval Certification. I won several prestigious awards in the automotive sector and held many of the records to this day in the industry!

Over the next five years, I grew my business to multiple eight figures before it came crashing down.

Friday, June 13th, 2008, was the day I received a call that shattered me. My wife had passed away. That was the moment I lost it. I mean, drugs, alcohol, and partying in excess. For a year and a half, I slid down the proverbial rabbit hole. I lost one hundred million dollars in cash, property, and assets; swirled down the drain.

I had met a girl in that period when I lost my mind boozing and drugging. A few months later she found out that she was pregnant, and I sobered up. Our son was born, and she moved in so we could try our hand at being a family. By the end of the month, I realized she had never actually sobered up. I came home one day and found her in the bed, passed out, and our baby was on the ground screaming and crying. There were pills and bottles everywhere.

I picked up my son, went to a hotel, and filed for custody that Monday. My last $100,000 in the bank went to fighting for control of my boy. Due to all the fighting in court, I ended up losing my contracts. Down to just thirty-two dollars and no longer able to afford a hotel, my son and I found ourselves homeless. We started sleeping in my car. Then came that dark moment.

Click.

The gun jammed, and after the third attempt, I remember thinking this is crazy! My son was asleep in the back seat, so I got out of the car, and I started screaming at the top of my lungs. I yelled, "F*ck you, show up!" to God. I was so pissed off and furious at Him. I was in an agonizing rage.

Gutted with grief, I fully understood that I was on this earth for a reason! I found Desire!

I got back into my car and closed my eyes to calm my breathing, and that's when I heard my son's voice. Even though he was a baby, sleeping undisturbed in the back, I heard him speak. I know babies don't talk at that age, but I listened to his voice so loud and clear. It's the same voice that he uses today when he yells down the stairs, "Hey Dad, can I go outside and play?" In that terrible and life-altering moment, I heard his child-filled voice speaking directly to me. And that voice said, "Daddy, everything's going to be okay."

I heard it clear as day, audibly, as if he were a wide-awake and confident young boy speaking lovingly and courageously to his father. I can honestly say I felt his presence, the caring child that would enrich my life and become my absolute best friend. He was right there with me in spirit and strength. I knew that giving him a beautiful life was part of my purpose and my desire!

Over the next few months, I started searching for a new business opportunity. I was determined to look at everything with an open mind, knowing that the right and perfect opportunity would arrive.

I discovered some unique loopholes while dabbling in real estate, and that started with me calling homeowners to see if they wanted to sell their house at a discounted rate. I began wholesaling real estate virtually because I couldn't drive all over Dallas with my son, so I did deals over the phone and by email. I conducted twenty-three transactions my first month, thirty-seven transactions in my second, and that's when I knew that I could build a new empire in real estate. I felt inspired again.

When the gun jammed, I knew my destiny was to be a father, husband, and leader who focuses on those in my direction. Over the last nine years, I've rekindled my relationship with my daughter, married an amazing woman, and have been recognized as an international keynote speaker who has spoken with some of the greatest minds in the world, the likes of Tai Lopez, Dr. Greg Reid, Les Brown, Dr. Eric Thomas, and Matt and Caleb Maddix to name a few. They have hired me to tell my story and teach the sales techniques in my five-step process.

I've learned I can overcome anything, and so can you! If you live life as if there's another explanation, you can see other massive opportunities with all kinds of possibilities. When you're in a shadow of life, there's always light coming from somewhere.

So, keep searching for the light. Let that fire inside of you sharpen your will. They now call me Coach Sharpen. So my friend, sharpen your skills and know that the best work you can do is the work that you do on you!

Whatever you do, do something! The minute you stop is when your subconscious plays all the tapes working against you! You don't have to be perfect; you should strive for progress. Don't stop. Keep searching. I hope you find your desire!

BRYCE MCKINLEY

About Bryce McKinley: Bryce is an International Best-Selling Author and one of the Top 5 Sales Trainers in the world, with over 20 years of working with various Fortune 500 companies including, but not limited to, the likes of Ford, Nissan, Tyco, and ADT. Helping each of them transform their sales process to focus on better conversations and building better relationships. Over 8,000 transactions in real estate, Bryce is one of the leading experts in wholesaling houses with his 5 Hour Flip method and has been able to close almost every deal over the phone, only ever walking 5 properties.

Author's website: *www.REIResultsAcademy.com*
Book Series Website & Author's Bio: *www.The13StepsToRiches.com*

HOW BADLY DO YOU WANT IT?

In the movie *Inside Out*, we are introduced to the idea that each one of us have little people controlling our actions. If we're happy, Joy has control, if angry, then Anger gets to drive. I'd like to simplify that down to just two: the driver and the passenger. How does our desire affect them and what they do?

Let's start with the passenger. Each of us have been a passenger at some point in our life. As a passenger, you get to ride along and enjoy things. It's easy to just sit there and let life happen around you, wishing and hoping for things, but never quite reaching them.

As a teenager, I had the dream to be a basketball player. My family didn't have the resources for me to join any of the little league basketball teams, so I spent my time playing with my friends at the park. I didn't really have any talent. But I knew if I practiced, I'd get better and reach my goal to be a ball player.

One spring, the local rec center offered a league that wouldn't cost any money to join. *Now's my chance*, I thought. I practiced even harder. The day of tryouts came. As I stepped onto the court,

I knew I was going to make it. As the tryout progressed, I was pushed to the side repeatedly by other boys, boys who wanted to play ball more than I did. The more I let them push me aside, the easier it became for me to just watch. At the end of the tryout, I wasn't offered a place on the team. I had let others decide my fate for me and taken a role as a passenger. I left that tryout defeated and gave up my dream to be a basketball player.

As a passenger, you may find or have many ideas or things that sound great. You just don't have the drive or burning desire to make those dreams and hopes a reality. As a driver, you have control. You decide which way to go. Unlike the passenger, you might miss some of the cool or pretty sights along the road, but that's because you're focused on the destination. You don't really have time for sidetracks.

That same spring, after losing my spot on the team, my band teacher approached the class and asked if anyone wanted to play the saxophone the next school year. I promptly raised my hand. I had been playing the clarinet for four years at that point and had wanted to play the sax. The teacher sent me home with books and a sax to learn to play it. I had a new goal to reach, and this time, I wasn't going to fail. So, as I took the saxophone home, I read the books my teacher had sent with me and started playing the instrument. It became an obsession for me. I was practicing constantly. By the end of summer break, I had taught myself how to play the sax, and when tryouts for the jazz band happened, I was able to perform well, and I made the band.

So, how do we stop being passengers and take control of the wheel and become the driver? First, you need to find something that you're passionate about and feed it. Feed your goals by learning everything you can about them. Read every book, blog, magazine, or news article you can find. As you do this, you will start to develop a burning desire to learn more, which will lead you to surround yourself with people you want to be like. You can't soar with the eagles if you're scratching with the chickens. I was told once, "You can't *change* the people around you, but you can change the *people* around you." Start looking at your social circle and eliminate negative, non-supportive people and fill that space with like-minded people.

Then, the hardest part is to take that first step. As Nike says, "Just do it." Grab the wheel and drive. Start small, but be consistent. Consistency is the key to longevity. Remember: it is easy to fall, and you will fall along the way. Don't let those missteps push you to the passenger seat. Instead, look for the victories and celebrate them. Even the small ones can help stimulate the driver and keep you moving forward.

~ David Rose

Desire—it's all about how badly you want it.

Many years ago, I was a young soldier. But not just a young soldier; I was a female soldier in a unit of one hundred plus males to approximately six females. We had a training exercise in another state, and an advanced party was needed to drive equipment. The party was to leave approximately one week before the main body. I wanted to be a part of the advance party, and to my surprise, I was met with staunch opposition.

I would be the only female going, and it would be almost one thousand miles spread out over several days. And as one officer pointed out, I "couldn't pee off a running board." Accommodating me was too inconvenient. I would slow them down and require too much babysitting. All these years later, I don't remember exactly what I said to convince them to give me a shot, but they did. I'm sure I cited something about equal opportunity. I was, after all, the Legal NCO for the unit.

Let's just say, "Where there's a will, there's a way!"

As a soldier. As a woman. As a mom. As an entrepreneur. As an adult. I have learned to be my own advocate. No one can advocate my best interests better than I can. And the answer is always "no" to the unasked question.

Desire is the key to unlock the unimaginable and unattainable. It is the first awareness of all things fulfilling. It lets the Universe home in on our unique place in a vast multitude of possibilities.

In October of 2020, I had an email come across my path inviting me to a "Courage to Be" retreat for women. I didn't know how it would change my life. Almost a year later, I can't imagine what my life would be like if I had not gone. But I had a burning desire to attend. And so, I did.

And that is all you need. Starting out is as simple as desiring to "do the next right thing" for you. To open the door and step through. From waking up every morning, to deciding what to do for the day. It doesn't exist without the desire to keep going. To grow, learn, and change.

Battles are won within, starting with desire. And as Shakespeare said in *Twelfth Night*, "Some are born into greatness. Some achieve greatness. And some have greatness thrust upon them." But despite what the Universe may bless you with upon your birth, it doesn't matter without the desire to use it and become it.

Whatever you may be facing at this very moment, whatever circumstances you are dealing with, if you aren't content with them, if you want them to change, you are already on your way. Let that "want" become a spark that ignites the flame of possibilities. Put one foot in front of the other and make it happen. As David said earlier in this chapter, small successes can stimulate the drive that makes the change sustainable. It doesn't take much. The basics of human nature, really.

My favorite book in the world has always been *The Places You'll Go*, by Dr. Seuss. If you haven't read it in a while, or if you don't own it, I recommend you pick it up and give it a read. My favorite part is the end:

> "So be your name Buxbaum or Bixby or Bray or Mordecai Ali Van Allen O'Shea, you're off to great places! Today is your day!" ~ Candace Rose

CANDACE & DAVID ROSE

About Candace and David Rose: They live in South Jordan, Utah with their 6 children, 6 chickens, 2 dogs, 2 cats, and rabbit. They both are Veterans of the US Army. David served as a Mechanic and Candace a Legal NCO. David is currently a Product Release Specialist, delivering liquid oxygen and nitrogen to various manufacturing plants and hospitals throughout Utah, Colorado, Idaho, and Nevada. Candace is the owner of Changing Your Box Coaching where she specializes in helping people organize their space, both physically and mentally. Both Candace and David are proud members of the elite Champion Circle Networking Association in Salt Lake City, Utah founded by one of our Co-Authors of *The 13 Steps to Riches* Book Series, Jon Kovach Jr.

Author's website: *www.ChangeYourBox.com*
Book Series Website & Author's Bio: *www.The13StepsToRiches.com*

Collier Landry

STARING DOWN DESIRE

When I was a freshman in music school, I took a class called Music Theory 101. This is standard curriculum for *every* freshman at any conservatory in the world. However, when you are a student who has never learned to actually *read* music, this can be a problematic and daunting course of study. Needless to say, I struggled terribly, and after my first week I found myself a staple at my professor's office hours asking rudimentary questions like, "What key are we in?" and "What note is that?" Being a seasoned musician of his stature, it was clear he found me both amusing and annoying simultaneously.

Professor Schroeder was a good-natured fellow, who seemed to oddly admire my persistence to overcome my learning curve. During one of our sessions, he abruptly stood up, walked to his office door, and removed his hanging jacket, revealing the following quote, often credited, *albeit mistakenly,* to philosopher Aristotle:

We are what we repeatedly do. Excellence, then, is not an act, but a habit.

Speaking softly through his bushy red mustache, he pointed and said, "Collier, despite your inability to actually read music and glaring lack of overall musical knowledge required for students to be accepted at this school, you do possess one quality other students here seem to lack."

"Really? What's that?" I replied, nervously preparing for another blow to my already fragile musical ego.

"You have the fire in the belly," he said with a subtle and endearing smile. "And that's a good thing."

I finished that year with a C+ average.

Despite my inevitable exodus from conservatory a few short years later, I never forgot that conversation. The truth is I always had the "fire in the belly," and I know precisely where that came from.

My mother, Noreen, was the second of two girls born into a working-class German-Irish immigrant family in suburban Philadelphia. She was a striking, refined, and poised woman with Eastern European features, platinum blonde hair, and piercing blue eyes. She had a sharp intellect and even sharper tongue. Despite her rather humble beginnings, my mother went on to earn a scholarship to one of the most prestigious young women's academies in all of Philadelphia. After graduating, she received a full scholarship to the University of Pennsylvania School of Dentistry, graduating a four-year program in just over three years.

Having grown up in the big, diverse city of Philadelphia, my mother had acquired a very unique perspective of the world. Although she came from a very humble working-class family, when attending boarding school, she was surrounded by young women who often came from more affluent families. My mother observed that things such as entitlement often stunted their motivation to succeed. It was here where she learned that applying the principles of hard work, dedication, and relentlessness to her studies would propel her to the life she ultimately desired.

By the time my family moved to a small town in Ohio, my mother was determined to teach me her "big city" philosophies. This is where she taught me the real meaning of what desire was and how to pursue it.

My mother's drive was always awe-inspiring to me, even when I was a small child. Since I was the only child, I was my mother's constant companion, always by my side and I by hers. I watched her balance managing a career, keeping our household in order, and leading a busy social life. She became completely immersed in everything that went on at the school I was attending, often being a school board member while maintaining her role in the bake sales and Christmas plays. Most important was the job she loved the most, which was raising a son with the value system she grew up with: hard work, passion, kindness, and integrity. My mother used to say, "Fire is lit with a match strike." If I was to ultimately become the man she knew I could be, I needed to figure out what would strike that fire inside *me*.

During her abbreviated tenure on this earth, my mother tirelessly reinforced my intellectual, creative, and personal independence. It wasn't until some twenty-five years later when I was making a documentary about her that I fully understood exactly how driven she was. I think most children look up to their parents as a sort of superhero and I was no different.

One of my fondest memories of her envisioning my future was when we were in a Nordstrom department store in Washington, D.C. Nordstrom was known for having pianists perform on weekends to entertain customers while they shopped. I was enthralled by the young man playing piano thinking, *How cool is this to sit in a tuxedo and play show tunes?!* My mother, observing my reaction to him playing and being that I already had a natural talent for all things musical, told me the following that evening at dinner.

"Collier, I think you should learn to play piano."

"That would be fun, Mommy," I said.

Encouraged by my enthusiasm, she continued, "That way, you will always have a job when you are going to law school at Georgetown!" I was enrolled in lessons once we returned home to Ohio.

Law school? Not so much. Toward the end of every school year, we would sit together at our kitchen table and select the courses of study I would take during my "summer vacation." While other kids were playing little league, going to the pool, or watching marathons of cartoons, I was taking advanced science classes, studying a second language and learning to throw pottery at the local arts center.

I suspect the motivation was equal parts my mother's desire to see me excel at everything I put my mind to and perhaps to have a few hours every day of summer to herself. I was, after all, an only child whose perpetual curiosity could test the patience of even the late Mother Teresa.

This book series is based on the thirteen principles Napoleon Hill outlines in his best-selling work, *Think and Grow Rich*. In today's world of Insta-fame, overnight millionaires, social media success stories, and the FOMO created from all these wonderful things, I'd like to examine the pursuit of riches and what that really means to me.

As a filmmaker, I have been a creative entrepreneur my entire adult life. That law school idea my mother put in my head when I was nine years old evaporated just as quickly. Professionals in the creative arts are often asked, "Why did you choose this line of work?" which is often followed with a canned response of, "I didn't choose it; it chose me." I find that to be just lip service, in my humble opinion.

The real reason is that you don't *have* a choice. I've found for myself that the burning desire to be a creative eclipses all things "responsible" like the job security of a traditional career and "playing it safe" life choices. You have to be at the point of no return; you flip the switch and have no option but burn the ships and forge ahead into the great unknown. As Sir Cecil Beaton poignantly stated, "Be daring, be different, be impractical, be anything that will assert integrity of purpose and imaginative vision against the play-it-safers, the creatures of the commonplace, the slaves of the ordinary."

If you can glean anything from my experiences in this chapter and those in the coming books in the series, first you will need to understand that your burning desire needs to be so much stronger than your FUD - *Fear - Uncertainty - Doubt*. Desire is what keeps me up at night, permeating my thoughts 24/7. And it should for you, too.

I have found over the course of my young life that *DESIRE* is the sum of *PASSION and DRIVE.* I learned drive from my mother, but my passion is what came from inside me. The burning desire to get out of small-town Ohio, to not become a victim of my circumstance. To find a better life that I truly desired to live. Artistic success is what I craved—not money. And don't get me wrong, money is a wonderful thing, but a journey exploring a life that truly ignites my soul every morning when my feet hit the floor is my desire.

I think the greatest gift any parent can bestow upon a child is to teach them to be a better version of themselves and give them the power to have courage to take that version and make it their own. Unbeknownst to me, my mother ingrained in me a foundation that would set me up to face, head-on, one of the most catastrophic sets of circumstances anyone, let alone an 11-year-old boy could be faced with.

When the time came for me to stare down the monster in front of me, that became *my* match strike moment.

And it would change the course of my life forever.

COLLIER LANDRY

About Collier Landry: As a formally trained musician and photographer, Collier Landry segued into filmmaking as a means to creatively express and deal with his own traumatic story—that of the murder of his mother by his father.

Subsequently, Collier is the creator and subject of Investigation Discovery's A Murder in Mansfield, a documentary directed by two-time Academy Award winner Barbara Kopple. Collier, who witnessed the murder at age 12, became the chief witness for the prosecution, returns to Ohio seeking to retrace his past and confront his father, who remains incarcerated and in denial of his guilt.

The film explores not only the collateral damage of violence and its traumatic repercussions, but the beauty of human strength and resilience through seemingly insurmountable odds.

Collier has been featured in *Variety, The New York Times, Esquire, USA Today,* is a TEDx Speaker, and guest on the *The Phil* show. He resides in Santa Monica, California.

Author's website: *www.CollierLandry.com*
Book Series Website & Author's Bio: *www.The13StepsToRiches.com*

Corey Poirier

AT THE FEET OF DESIRE

In 2016, I released *The Book of WHY and HOW*. The idea behind the book was to help people discover their calling and then share with them what I've learned after interviews with more than 6,500 influencers about how to leverage your "why" to do great things. In the book, I referred often to passion and purpose. I noted that passion is what you do (e.g. photography) and purpose is why you do it (e.g. to help people capture their legacy moments).

I explained that when I interviewed former professional wrestler Trish Stratus, I wanted to know why The Rock, Stone Cold Steve Austin, and Hulk Hogan were known better than anyone else in that industry. I asked her what the common trait was among them, considering she had spent time with each. She shared with me that it was their level of passion.

As someone who has read *Think and Grow Rich* many times, I discovered as I prepared to write this chapter that I hadn't fully immersed myself in the chapter on *desire* enough as I was thinking that I would be writing about passion and using it interchangeably with *desire*. Then, I reflected on my definition of *desire*, only to realize it is yet a separate thing from passion.

I realized that if passion is what you do and purpose is why you do, desire is how you want to do it. Do you want it bad enough to make the necessary sacrifices? I realized for the first time these are different things.

If you're passionate about something, you typically love to do it and won't watch the clock, but it doesn't mean you keep the visual in your head and think about doing it daily. I love playing guitar and writing music. Yet, even though I love doing it, I don't visualize and think about doing it daily. I'm also not sure I'd be willing to make many sacrifices these days to do it either. So, it may be a passion, and I may have a purpose in doing it, but it's not a driving *desire*.

Now, to go back to my conversation with Trish and her comment that their level of passion for wrestling was at an all-time high, on reflection now, I'm guessing their *desire* to do it was also at an all-time high, and maybe that is what separated them from the other wrestlers who simply had a lot of passion. This awakening around *desire* for me is a big deal.

To give you an example of how big of an impact *Think and Grow Rich* had on me, it was the second book I read at age twenty-seven and it not only changed my life, but years later, when I had the opportunity to interview Bob Proctor for the first time and held his fifty-seven year old copy of *Think and Grow Rich* in my hand, I was like a kid in a candy store. I imagine it was like someone feels when they hold the master copy of their favorite band's album in their hands.

Yet, when I reflected on writing this chapter, I realized I didn't fully know my own definition of the word *desire*. Now that I have my definition firmly in hand, let me share my own *desire* with you, and then perhaps a few stories from my years of interviewing influencers—as both are related.

I have multiple *desires* but the one that is by far the biggest is this: interviewing people and sharing what I have learned during those interviews. I can't imagine not interviewing people. I do think about interviewing people regularly and even visualize how the interview will go. I have been working with James Redfield (Celestine Prophecy) on a documentary recently, and in deciding who I wanted to interview for the project, I even set up a vision board with the faces of the interviewees on it.

I'm also passionate about it of course, and I feel when I'm doing it, I am living on purpose, but it is also a *desire*. I look to Hill's words in the chapter on *desire* when he says "Barnes's *desire* was not a *hope*! It was not a *wish*! It was a keen, pulsating *desire*, which transcended everything else. It was definite." This is how I feel about interviewing people and learning the common traits they share, the setbacks they have experienced, and the lessons they have learned.

My girlfriend would be the first to tell you this. She would tell you quickly how much I light up when I share my experience during the most recent interview, and how disappointed I get when we have to reschedule an interview—even though I know the Universe rescheduled it for a good reason.

Realizing this is such a desire in my life has made writing this chapter a big win for me; however I want this to be about you and how you can figure out what your biggest desire is, and so I'd like to share a few stories before I close and then ask you a simple question.

Two weeks ago, I interviewed UFC Legend Ken Shamrock. He spoke about how he came from a broken home, and often ended up in street fights. He talked about running away from home at an early age and being stabbed by another runaway. Kicked out at a young age by his stepfather, he ended up living in cars before ending up in foster homes. He ultimately found himself in a home for boys operated by Bob Shamrock. At this point, Ken was still aggressive and acting out. Bob ultimately realized that Ken excelled at sport and involving him in sport would be a productive way to get his aggression out. Almost immediately, Ken found his purpose, his passion, *and* he began to think about sport on the regular and visualize his fights, and ultimately, have a powerful *desire* to excel at the highest level.

He has since become one of the most well-known MMA fighters in the world, while also becoming a well-known professional wrestler. I truly believe it's because he had such a strong *desire* to reach the top level in something he was so drawn to.

Now, consider this. Lisa Nichols, widely known from *The Secret*, being the face of MindValley, her Oprah appearances, being involved in the *Chicken Soup for the African American Soul* books, and being one of the world's top speakers struggled for years before finding something she *desired*. She struggled to buy diapers for her son at one point while on social assistance, and has since gone on to reach almost eighty million people while becoming a wealthy business owner and thought leader. She told me the change happened when she asked herself, *What if I expect something better?* In her words, "I was trying to outrun fear, trying to outrun broke, trying to outrun hurt, trying to outrun victim… but I was bold enough, I was brave enough, I was crazy enough to ask—what if I expect something better?" I believe it was Lisa's *desire* for something better that propelled her to literally change the world while impacting millions of people.

Finally, another illustration is that of John Gray, the author of *Men are from Mars*. John literally had me in disbelief telling me how for eight years, EVERY SINGLE DAY, he set an intention for his book series to become the bestselling relationship book series, in hopes that he could impact as many lives as possible. To date, the number varies, but I've heard figures as high as 100 million copies sold. His intentions paid off, but here's the thing: if he didn't have a *desire* to impact that many lives, would he have committed to setting an intention every single day, even on those days where perhaps the book didn't sell many copies? I believe it was John's *desire* to help people in their relationships that helped him visualize it, and intend it, on the daily.

I could literally share thousands of stories of what became possible at the feet of *desire*, but instead, I'd like you to instead consider what it is you *desire*? What is it you want so badly that it transcends everything else?

The main question I wanted to ask you is this: Are you ready to start the work to figure out what it is you *desire* so much that you'll do it passionately and with purpose?

If not, who will?

If so, I can't wait to hear all about it!

COREY POIRIER

About Corey Poirier: Corey Poirier is a multiple-time TEDx Speaker. He is also the host of the top-rated *Let's Do Influencing* radio show, founder of The Speaking Program, founder of bLU Talks, and has been featured in multiple television specials. He is also a Barnes and Noble, Amazon, Apple Books, and Kobo Bestselling Author and the co-author of the *Wall Street Journal / USA Today* bestseller, *Quitless.*

A columnist with *Entrepreneur* and *Forbes* magazine, he has been featured in/on various mediums and is one of the few leaders featured twice on the popular *Entrepreneur on Fire* show.

He has also interviewed over 6,500 of the world's top leaders and he has spoken on-site at Harvard and more recently to Microsoft team leaders and at inner circle retreats, which has featured everyone from Brian Tracy to Mark Victor Hansen to Phil Collen (Def Leppard).

Also appearing on the popular Evan Carmichael YouTube Channel, he is a New Media Summit Icon of Influence, was recently listed as the # 5 influencer in entrepreneurship by Thinkers 360, and he is an Entrepreneur of the Year Nominee—and, to demonstrate his versatility, a Rock Recording of the Year nominee who has performed stand-up comedy more than 700 times, including an appearance at the famed Second City.

Author's website: *www.TheInfluencerVault.com*
Book Series Website & Author's Bio: *www.The13StepsToRiches.com*

David Nicholson

DESIRE TO LOVE YOURSELF FIRST

Moments before I planned to end my life, my phone alerted me of a text message. It read, "Dad, I need you..."

Throughout my life, I've had an unhealthy driving want to please other people. However, a desire is a lot deeper than just a mere want. To want something wrong enough, it must have an emotion or feeling backing it. A passion that drives you to take action for something is the true power behind this step to personal freedom.

I haven't pursued my true desires until now–only my wish to please and be there for other people. It's an interesting dichotomy that my wishing oversaw my passion for purpose and belonging to please everybody else. I forgot about what was essential, so I've recently made many changes in my life to pursue my true desires; I'm making myself happy and whole.

My life-long desires don't necessarily keep me from doing things that would please others. What I'm trying to do is not selfish, but I've found that I'm better able to help others on their journey through pursuing my desires. My desires inspire others to follow their desires. The more you help others, you too will seek your desires. Then you become a driving force that enables people towards their passions, and that's a kind of selfless giving that is contagious.

My driving desire has driven me to change the world and bring self-love back to the forefront of people's lives, including my own. My daily technique of getting self-love back starts with me telling myself what I love about myself. Sharing things that I love about myself has improved my gratitude and energy, allowing me to serve others.

For example, I recently spent a week in a hospital and a week on bed rest because I had not been taking care of myself physically and medically the way my doctors had advised me. I was stuck in a small-town hospital in Southern Utah, hundreds of miles from my home. Therefore, I didn't have friends or family that could visit. Feeling alone, stuck and hopeless, I didn't know if I would make it out of the hospital. Those days were long and challenging.

The one thing that helped me heal physically and mentally was my focus on the desire to share self-love with myself and others–it is my life mission. I learned to love myself even more while on that hospital bed. I exercised my technique every day by sharing something new that I love about myself. It helped me to get through that trial and ultimately recover fast enough to be dismissed from the hospital in a matter of weeks.

I would advise you, reading this now, as if I were advising my younger self to focus on the self-love technique. Focus on writing, journaling, or even speaking aloud the things that you love about yourself. Visualize taking care of yourself. It is not selfish. It is necessary. It took me years of my life to realize this.

To help other people, we first have to be healthy ourselves. If you genuinely desire to help or make those around you happy and healthy and help them fulfill their desires, you first have to be happy and healthy and love yourself. And like I said, I spent decades trying to make everybody else happy.

The more I've discovered how much I love myself, I've expanded my capacities to take on more ventures. I recently took on a new full-time job, and I drive a lot with Uber and Lyft. I've even taken on professional development projects that consume my time and days. However, I suddenly slipped back into the habit of taking on too much and trying to help others before myself—even things as simple as taking my medications for severe medical conditions. Not checking on my physical health landed me in that remote hospital, and the doctors forced me to sit back, recover and focus on myself. Things could have ended badly, but my self-love technique accelerated my recovery and got me back out on the road working again.

It's one thing for me to tell myself that I love myself and vocalize that, but if I'm not doing the basic activities that will keep me happy and healthy, then it's all for nothing. A significant desire for self-love has expanded into my physical health and wellbeing.

How can I possibly say that I love myself and then let my body fall apart? That must be a big focus right now for all who need increased recovery. It's helping my mental health and physical health. As I feel better physically, I'll feel better mentally again, which is the opposite of what most personal development mentors are saying these days. I'll be around longer to help my loved ones chase after their desires too. I'm alive and well today because of my desire to teach self-love and for my children, who remind me of my purpose.

A dark time in my life became the most significant because it taught me this important principle for desiring self-love. One evening, I prepared to take my life. It was a text message from my son that kept me from going through with it in that darkest moment. As I find myself slipping in other areas of my life, it's thoughts of my children that bring me back. Even though I haven't been the most considerable influence of self-love, that all has changed.

As I sat there, ready to take my life, a text message came in. I only got through the first three words. The text was from my son. He had texted me miraculously before I was able to end my life. The text read, "Dad, I need you... to pick me up." But I didn't get to read the whole thing before the tears came, and I couldn't read anything beyond that first phrase, "Dad, I need you..." Those four words were enough to help me come to my senses and realize that they do need me and that I have belonging and purpose in life. There would have been a lot missing in their lives had I gone through with it.

My son needed me, which meant that others depended on me. I had a purpose. I belonged to something important, which was the source of my self-love, self-worth, and personal happiness. My darkest hour quickly transitioned into the brightest enlightening moment in my entire life. The realization that my purpose relied heavily on the fact that others needed me was the turning point.

You, too, have purpose and belonging. By learning to love yourself, you shall help others perpetuate self-love throughout the world and through generations to come.

DAVID NICHOLSON

About David Nicholson: David is a consummate professional with over 20+ years of experience as an IT Consultant in Windows-based networking. David has worked for a large array of companies including small businesses up to multi-national corporations. His experience covers a wide spectrum of technologies including: Windows Servers and Workstations, Wireless Protocols, Remote Desktop Services, Virtual Private Networking and Remote Access, MS Exchange Server, MS SQL Server, SAN & NAS Storage Solutions, Mobile Devices, and Multiple Backup Solutions. David is a successful network administrator. On several occasions, David learned and provided industrial controls networking and programming within a tight turnaround. David is a master programmer. He is an extremely knowledgeable network, Active Directory and Exchange administrator.

Author's website: *www.facebook.com/dlnicholson*
Book Series Website & Author's Bio: *www.The13StepsToRiches.com*

Deb Scott

IT WAS DESIRE

Think and Grow Rich states the very first step to "think and grow rich" is desire. Desire is the seed that holds the genetics and potential for everything else to create your success.

It was desire that motivated me to turn my sexual abuse by a teacher in school to become a Sunday school volunteer and, ultimately, director of Confirmation with eighty fifteen-year-olds to inspire to gain Godly discernment between good and evil. I wanted those young people to avoid the pain and suffering I experienced from being naïve of pedophiles.

It was desire that brought me to become a member of the Regis College swim team as the only person who made the team without prior competitive background and later became elected co-captain.

It was desire that allowed me to be an national award-winning cardiac surgical sales rep in the Boston area for over two decades.

It was desire that gave me the strength to be the sole caregiver (only child) for both my parents, who passed away within a year of each other from cancer.

It was desire to be a better person and help others that motivated me to become a Certified Life Coach.

It was desire that got me out of a verbally abusive relationship with an alcoholic man I was engaged to and got me into Al-Anon, where I learned healthy boundaries.

It was desire that allowed me to fight back after losing one million dollars in one of the biggest Ponzi schemes with a fake Millennium bank in 2009.

It was Desire that allowed me to take all my mother's and grandmother's vintage items as I was cleaning out the family home I had to sell and turn it into a vintage clothing store in Newburyport called "A Little Bit of Rachel," named after and in honor of my mother.

It was Desire that created a way to cash out my retirement to pay for heat and water in my house to survive until I could sell it and begin a new life after losing one million dollars.

It was desire that motivated me to take my personal experiences and share them in a book which became a motivational bestseller on Amazon and a four-time award-winning book, including the INDIE Next Generation Award in New York City – *The Sky is Green & The Grass is Blue – Turning Our Upside Down World Right Side Up.*

It was desire that motivated me to create a podcast *The Best People We Know Show* to help people gain hope that anything is possible, which was top rated in twenty-five categories and became a Shorty Award Winner in New York City.

It was desire that helped me to sell my 1835 family home in the North Shore of Boston and move to a town I had never heard of, and where didn't know a soul: Venice, Florida. I just knew I needed to find warm weather, my dog, and a palm tree to speak with.

It was desire that got me to change careers and become a licensed Realtor in Florida, because that is what my father, mother, and grandfather did back in the Boston area. In my second year, I became a top producer in Sarasota County with EXP Realty.

It was desire that brought me to the present moment. The desire to help anyone and everyone believe in their heart desire is the initial key necessary to economic and/or spiritual wealth. The first step to success and good change is desire.

My desire is to take anything bad and transform it into something great. This is why I joined in the writing of this book series.

How do you know or get desire?

I sit quietly and pray for discernment and direction. If I feel peace, I move towards my goal. If I feel confusion, I walk away from the goal.

I trust that God has given me special talents to do a specific job that only I can do. And this is true for you. If you are alive, you have a purpose, a job which no one else can complete the exact way you can, to accomplish the goal planted deep inside your heart.

The point with desire is that you do not have to understand the how or why, you just have to identify and believe and trust. The result and how your desire manifests is what we will discuss in the following chapters.

Sometimes, God will use what we perceive to be bad things in our life to move us towards our goal. For example, if I had not lost one million dollars, I would probably still be in the family back in the North Shore of Boston and never go back to work. I would be comfortable, and comfortable is a close cousin to being complacent.

Losing that million dollars forced me to face the truth of who I was, my priorities, what mattered in this life, what I wanted the rest of my life to look like, how I wanted to feel, who I wanted to be with, and how to be a better friend with myself. It also taught me humility, compassion, and forgiveness in a way so powerful I can actually say as much as I hated losing it, I am a better person for having lost it.

If not for losing that million dollars, I would never have had the courage to move. And not just move anywhere, but to a place that was warm with palm trees, because that was my desire. I originally thought that place was Clearwater, but when I went there, nothing was right. It was confusion. I came home totally disappointed.

Then, a friend told me about the Sarasota and Venice area. Venice? Like Venice, Italy? I laughed, because I never heard of such a place. But when I researched homes in the Sarasota and Venice area that would accept a dog, I came down to two homes to rent. One in Sarasota and one in Venice. The Venice owner negotiated with me, so I signed a lease to move into a house in Venice I had never seen. I had never been to the town, didn't know a soul, and had no idea what I would do for work. I just trusted my desire to move there.

Three years later, I can say I love living here. I still miss the Boston area, but what I really miss is the life and people I had there, and they are all gone. My family has all passed away, and I must accept change and be grateful for my past and trust God has a great plan for my future. I have the desire to live a happy, peaceful, and purposeful life. I have the desire to help everyone I meet achieve the same.

This is the desire that feeds my soul to good change. This is the desire that makes a crazy thought a genius solution. This is the desire that has always allowed me to do the impossible in my life. This is the desire I want you to have to make your dreams come true.

I often reflect on the first man who ran a four-minute mile. No one had ever done this before, and the experts said it was impossible. Then one day, someone did it. He actually ran the mile in four minutes. And you know what happened after that? More people ran a four-minute mile.

Now, was it a physical change in their body or their mind that allowed all these other people to do what the first person accomplished? It's always impossible until it's done.

The next steps are a beautiful journey with all these amazing people, just like you, who want to help you make desire happen for you, too.

We aren't finished yet—let's go.

DEB SCOTT

About Deb Scott: Deb Scott, BA, CPC, and Realtor was a high honors biology major at Regis College in Weston, Massachusetts, and spent over two decades as an award-winning cardio-thoracic sales specialist in the New England area. She is a best-selling author of The Sky is Green & The Grass is Blue: Turning Your Upside Down World Right Side Up. She is an award-winning podcaster of The Best People We Know Show. Following in her family's footsteps, she is a third generation Realtor in Venice, Florida. As a certified life coach, Deb speaks and teaches on how to turn bad situations into positive, successful results. As a top sales specialist, she enjoys teaching people "sales without selling," believing that integrity, good communication, and respect are the winning equation to all outstanding success and happiness in life.

Author's website: *www.DebScott.com*
Book Series Website & Author's Bio: *www.The13StepsToRiches.com*

Dori Ray

A MOVE TOWARD DESIRE

I lifted my head to the ceiling. I was sitting on the last box in my living room. Another chapter was ending badly. For the third time in ten years as a single parent of two daughters, I was ending a chapter with the last sentence reading, "Please remove all of your personal belongings and return the keys to the main office."

Once again, depression had won! I was exhausted from this round! This one was super-hard. Everybody was watching, and I had let them down, again. The people pleaser in me was having a particularly bad day; however, this time, something felt peculiar. At the base of all this pain was something a little different. This time I felt like it was time that should become a must. I was taught in my career that when a should becomes a must, we activate the impossible and create miracles. I needed a miracle!

My desire to be well was more intense than ever! Being sick was no longer an option! It was costing too much. If I had to pay a price anyway, I would rather pay one that will free my mind. My desire to be well was no longer an option. The should had become a must! I could no longer allow depression to steal my joy, my peace, my dreams, my gifts, my life. Something had changed and I felt it.

I remember back when she first showed up. It's so crazy to think, she had given me a warning that she was on her way. I had just finished reading a textbook to learn how to sell antidepressants for a pharmaceutical company I was working for at the time. I should have recognized her immediately. But I had never had any issues with her. I had seen her ruin many lives, but she wouldn't touch me, The Chosen One. Everybody loved me! I had more friends than Raymond!

I remember the day she knocked on my door. You know, that ugly, unforgiving, uncaring, rude one who shows up without calling, stays longer than welcomed, and never cleans up her mess! She introduced herself as Depression. I learned early on that there was no way depression could be of the male persuasion. She was just too crafty! I had never seen a man move with such precision!

"D," the name I gave her on her third visit when my girls were little, slithered her way in and out of my life for almost two decades. She always showed up when I was at the top of my game. She was so crafty that no one would even see her coming. My mom didn't even see her, and my Mother was the self-proclaimed nosiest woman alive.

It was as if she had keys to everything I owned. I knew I had to stop her before she took over my life. I was determined not to let that evil woman just throw me around. She had already taken fifteen years, and there was nothing left for her. I was sick of cleaning up after her, sick of her stealing my hours, days, weeks, months, and years. I decided to whip her tail.

But then, after a quick thought, I said, "No, the only way she won't return is if I kill her." Killing "D" was not going to be easy, but it would definitely be worth it. I had to count the cost, consider the price I was willing to pay, and rule out any and all other options. I knew it was going to be a long process. I was willing to do whatever it took. I would do whatever the Universe suggested, as long as the end result was peace and love. That day, I made a definite decision and wrote the following letter on a piece of paper I found in my pocketbook:

I deserve to be well. My daughters deserve a fun, happy, healthy mom. I deserve to be in a loving relationship. I deserve to have money to live the way I enjoy. I deserve a big team and to have all my dreams come true. The children and I deserve a vacation every year. My daughters deserve to live in a loving home, without the threat of being evicted at any moment. Nothing will stop me from having this. I will chase my dreams and beat depression. This time next year, people will not be able to recognize me.

Looking over this letter, it's crazy to see that the last line in a letter to myself was caring about what other people thought. If hindsight is 20/20, I now know why the eleven-day journey turned into a forty year escapade!

I decided to take my good friend up on her offer to move to California. I would take my younger daughter with me. She was entering eleventh grade, and little did I know depression had already assigned a close family member to her. I would leave my oldest child behind. This would be her first time apart from us. Leaving her in the hands of my biggest supporter made the decision a little easier, but it was still so difficult. My baby was only a sophomore in college and had just fallen in love for the first time.

My older daughter's voice startled me as she said, "C'mon, Mom, we gotta get going. We need to get to the storage unit before it closes." I turned around and looked at her with my manufactured smile and said, "Okay, baby." She turned to leave, and I called out to her, "Hey, everything is going to be okay." She never turned to look at me. She had heard that line too many times before, and she—like her little sister—was losing hope that their mom would ever be well. She later told me that she and her sister were preparing to take care of me for the rest of their lives. Just the thought of that broke me into pieces. However, it made me read that note one more time. As a matter of fact, I read it out loud, over and over and over, until I felt the tears streaming down my face.

I didn't even realize I had begun to scream. When I looked up, both of my children were looking me in my face. Their eyes were full of fear. It was a level of fear I had never seen. They thought I was losing it. Finally, Mommy had lost her mind. They had no idea that Mommy had finally found it! Without even knowing it, I had made a definite decision that depression had stolen her last moment. I was moving to California, and I would start my life over.

The Universe had been sitting back watching all this play out. He saw the internal struggle and could even document the moment where the magic happened. He wished he could show her the whole journey. He really loved her. She was strong. He knew, but she didn't. She was called. He knew, but she didn't. She was different.

She knew she was different, but was always uncomfortable with this unable to embrace and enjoy her differences. She had yet to discover and embrace how uniquely she was made for her special assignment.

The Universe chuckled as she finally got up off the box after sitting there for a full ten minutes! He watched her turn the key in the door for the last time with the last box in one hand, the letter and keys in the other. Little did I know even after I left the main office, I was still holding one of the keys that would transform my life: the letter. The journey was just beginning, and I had no idea the doors I would have to go through for every word in the letter to come true, but I did know there was no turning back. I made plans to leave right after the holidays and start my life over in a different place. I was taught that to have something different, you must do something different.

I called my friend and said, "Let's do it!" It never occurred to me to wonder why she was more excited than I was about starting my life over, only later to find out she was part of the test that I had to pass to make sure my dreams and desires written on that piece of paper would come true. I had made up my mind that there were no other options. My girls and I deserved a good life, and it was my job to create it!

After leaving the rental office, my daughters and I jumped in the U-Haul and drove to Philly. We sang our favorite songs and pretended everything was good. "Oh you gotta have faith, faith, faith."

DORI RAY

About Dori Ray: Dori "On Purpose" Ray is a native Philadelphian. As a business woman her mission is to help people transform their minds, bodies, and bank accounts!

Dori was educated in the Philadelphia Public School System. She graduated from the Philadelphia High School for Girls in 1982 and Howard University School of Business in 1986 with a BBA in Marketing. Dori is a member of De. Sigma Pi Business Fraternity and Delta Sigma Theta Sorority, Inc.

Dori leads teams around the world. She is a sought-after Speaker and Trainer within her industry and beyond. She is an experienced Re-Entry Coach as she has helped hundreds of Returning Citizens get back on track after incarceration.

Having suffered from depression for 20 years, she always reaches back to share her story and help break the cycle of silence. Her audience loves her authenticity.

Book Dori for speaking engagements www.linktr.ee/dorionpurpose

Author's website: *www.Linktr.ee/DoriOnPurpose*
Book Series Website & Author's Bio: *www.The13StepsToRiches.com*

Elaine Sugimura

MY MOXIE

From a very young age, I craved the opportunity to be a top performer amongst the pack, whether it was with education, sports, or my friendships. The very first opportunity for me presented itself when my kindergarten teacher, Ms. Moon, asked the class who was going to be the naptime captain. I raised my hand, and there I found myself taking a "big sister" role by supporting my classmates who often struggled with naptime. I so wanted to be a big sister, as I was the youngest of three.

I continued to step up in my youth whenever there was an opening to lead. Often, my desire to be the best was met with disdain. I had a tendency to step on other classmates' toes, literally, and found myself losing friends, rather than gaining them. This did not stop me; I continued to lead and wanted to be in everyone's favor, especially with my parents, teachers, and those with authority. I soon became known as the Asian girl with a lot of moxie and was asked to step down and allow others a chance to show their colors. Quietly, I decided to continue my quest to be a powerful leader, no matter what it took to get there.

By high school, I found my place and chose to concentrate on completing high school early and to start my life as a young, mature adult. Life was good... I had an amazing time, dating a few guys and working and earning cash to pay operating costs for my newly minted white Chevy Camaro I had earned for achieving straight A's throughout my high school education. Yes, life was happening to me, and it felt great. Of course, the next step was to begin my college career and with it new leadership challenges. This is where the foundation for the coming years would be set.

Well, what happened next was not exactly what I had planned. I met the love of my life at eighteen years old, and I felt like I had been hit by the love train. The energy and excitement I felt was like nothing I had ever experienced. I actually pinched myself and realized something was about to change the path that I had strategized and planned for oh so long.

I met Hiro at a part-time job I had prior to starting my college career. Our first encounter was like the day when I was five years old and was at the candy store; I knew this was a flavor I wanted and desired so much that I was willing to do anything to bag it up and take it home. I remember he entered wearing his tight Jimmy Conners white tennis shorts and Sergio Tacchini terry cloth shirt with flip flops. If you know anything about me, I am a fashionista, and somehow, his appearance did not matter. It was his being that I fell in love with.

Yes, love at first sight. I remember that day vividly. This was the moment I knew something was about to shift in my life. The rest is a story of desire that has led me down a road that allowed me to experience cravings that go beyond the initial sugar rush. Like dipping strawberries in melted chocolate, my heart melted at the sight and smell of this beautiful human. It was the first time I understood what it meant to trust your heart, to jump in, and to go for it, no matter the cost.

What happened next is all hell broke loose. Hiro and I found ourselves in the middle of a family feud. I left home to live in the cab-over camper that we purchased to travel the United States. I left behind my life as I knew it, an accomplished eighteen-year-old who was supposed to start the predetermined next chapter of her life. The detour sign was just ahead. My family was in turmoil, and I fought every step of the way and stayed the course, starting my new life with the man I fell in love with, who was now my only option.

As difficult as it was, I chose this life, as I was head over heels in love and craved a safe relationship, as home never felt safe for me, a story for another time. Life as I knew it was no longer the same. I chose to work three jobs to take responsibility for my life, and to prove that I was strong and smart enough to make the choices that were best for me. After a year of healing, I finally went back home, and my father finally accepted our relationship. I quickly learned that when I stood my ground, proved my reasoning, and fought for what I craved, anything is possible.

Life was moving fast. I got married, had two babies within four years, and my career as a fashionista began. I was not willing to give up on my dreams; my vision of becoming an accomplished businesswoman was next on my list. I learned that when you fight for what you desire, you can cause or manifest what truly brings joy, love, and inspiration to your life, family, and most of all YOU. I worked long hours to prove my worth, knowing that I did not have the same experiences as those around me.

My career spanned from sales to merchandising to running entire organizations to ultimately becoming a CEO in the fashion industry. I had broken through the glass ceiling. As an Asian-American woman, I was a minority in the industry, and to have achieved this career pinnacle in my life was immensely rewarding. Most importantly, it was an aha moment that anything is possible if you believe in yourself.

I moved on to become an entrepreneur. I now own and lead my own consulting company. For the last decade, I have continued to take risks and become a change-maker, figuring out ways to continue building the blocks to the foundation of my crazy and colorful life. There is still more to come, and I sense my work will be centered on the word "inspiration." Being inspiring to others is just as important as being inspired, and I want to live the rest of my life inspired by everything around me.

My life has been filled with both so many highs and lows. As a two-time breast cancer survivor, I had to learn how to not only survive, but thrive. At twenty-nine and forty-one years of age, I battled the voices in my head that kept saying, *You may not live, so create small wins that will allow you to conquer the fear of death.* I had only one goal at that moment in time: to see my children graduate from high school, and I did all I could to manifest that vision so it would come true. Not just once, but twice in my life.

As I reflect back at what I have shared here, each and every moment, big or small, reveals key lessons. I now can share these lessons to inspire others to hear, see, and take action for themselves. When we truly desire something and we do everything humanly possible to make it happen, we get to create the space to make it happen. Never give up just because someone else tells you it is not possible. I so wanted to be a leader at all costs, in all areas of my life, to manifest a way of life that would allow me to be a guide in the sky that symbolizes the fire from the sun.

I am reborn with the rising of the sun! A new blank canvas will be painted by my loving wings, and how beautiful will each painting be at the end of each colorful day. One step at a time, one moment at a time, supporting those who are merely surviving to thriving is where my next journey will take me.

One last share that is so near and dear to my heart. I want you all to know I am still madly in love with my Hiro, as he is "the wind beneath my wings!" Forty-one years after our first date, there is not a day that goes by that I am not grateful to the young me who never gave up on my true love. No matter how difficult it was, we made it, we created our beautiful family, we made our families whole, we each achieved our goals, we continue to love one another and hold each other high, and we are ONE.

I will continue to dare and lead a fulfilling life, no matter how difficult it becomes. The Game of Life, as I know it, is worth playing each and every day!

"Success is loving life and daring to live it."
– Maya Angelou

ELAINE SUGIMURA

About Elaine R. Sugimura: Elaine is an accomplished fashion executive turned entrepreneur who has a passion to create leaders amongst leaders. Currently, she owns several businesses and as CEO, she runs a franchise food and beverage organization that requires both strategy and execution. Fun fact: she is an adrenaline junkie—the higher, the faster, the better. Her love for adventure has led her to travel to many parts of the world by plane and automobile. She and her husband, Niro, share their home in Northern California. They have raised two extraordinary sons and have added two beautiful daughters-in-law to their growing family.

Author's website: *www.ElainerSugimura.com*
Book Series Website & Author's Bio: *www.The13StepsToRiches.com*

Elizabeth Walker

WHEN SHAPES IN THE CLOUDS ARE NOT JUST SHAPES

As a child, I would gaze in wonder at the sky. My favorite time to do this was not when other children would look up into the sky, looking at clouds, making shapes, and telling stories. My favorite time to gaze into the sky was during the darkness—particularly in the wee hours of the morning—to look at the sparkling stars and wonder. Was it just a dark curtain and the light was behind it shining through those little holes, or was it something more? I wondered what it was that those stars would deliver? Did they mean anything? Or were they there purely for my visual enjoyment and to stimulate my ever-evolving imagination?

As I watched those stunning stars shoot across the sky, twinkling slowly and sometimes faster, I began creating a belief that there was something much bigger than me leading the way. What is interesting about that is even now, in my fourth decade, I enjoy looking up at the night sky and can spend hours gazing into the great space. I can make sense of the constellations, and I can make sense of the movement of the sky, and I can make sense of what Galileo was pondering as he discovered Jupiter's moons: Io, Europa, Ganymede, and Callisto.

You may be wondering, and it is a good thing to wonder, what any of this has to do with DESIRE. The word "desire" comes from the Latin *De Sidere*, "await what the stars will bring." Some people are happy to sit in their status quo, whilst others embrace and embody desire.

Imagine the Lakes District in England, a series of small towns scattered around the edge of a large lake system where William Wordsworth, poet and author of "I Wandered Lonely as a Cloud" made his home. The Lakes District was the very place I first experienced desire in a way that was undeniable. I wandered lonely, as a 16-year-old girl who had left her high school sweetheart behind in Australia, to travel the U.K. with her parents. I wandered in and out of laneways and small shops and stumbled across a divine silver ring.

At the time, I wore rings on all of my fingers, and I was obsessed with fine silver. This particular ring was highly polished silver and was a zig-zag shape, so it formed the open symbol for water when worn. I had diligently saved my money from my part-time job prior to leaving Australia, knowing there would be at least one ring on the journey that I would desire. I purchased the ring, much to my parent's dismay and disappointment. They argued that it was too expensive, and I was wasting my hard-earned money. I purchased the ring, regardless of their opinion, and I wore it with pride, knowing that there was something special about the way it had been handcrafted and knowing that it was one-of-a-kind.

The ring remained with me for the duration of the trip around the U.K. and Europe, and it became an important part of who I was. It was a talking point with the many people I met, and the desire

I had for it when I first saw it was still present every time I looked down at my fingers.

We arrived back in Australia a few months later, and a few months after that, I was in our downstairs playroom dancing with my sister and some friends and looked down to find that the ring was missing. I was devastated. I knew that the ring was on my finger when we started dancing, as I had shown one of the girls who I had not seen since my return. The ring had to be in that room, and my desire to find that ring was phenomenal.

I started by deciding I was not going to stop looking until I had found the ring or emptied the entire room. I empowered myself by enlisting the help of others and looking in all the obvious places. Dolls' cots, Matchbox car garages, under televisions, under couches, and in my mother's sewing drawers, to no avail. The ring was nowhere to be found. I raised my standards, and piece by piece, I cleared out that room, searching for my beloved ring. I shook out every piece of cloth and tipped out every container. It was not there, and yet it was impossible that it was anywhere else.

I felt defeated momentarily, then I was literally inspired. I took a breath. I continued to search, and finally all that was left in the room was the carpet. So, I responded accordingly and set about scanning the carpet with my hands, whilst crawling on my knees, one twenty centimeter square at a time. After a few hours of mapping the floor and going grid by grid, the ring was still nowhere to be found. I continued my quest; the desire to have that ring was overwhelming. Rather than stop with that overwhelm, I kept going and going and going. By 11:00 p.m. that night, I had started to lift up all the edges of the carpet, in case it had fallen down under the skirting boards. I responded to my own disappointment and decided to sleep until morning, gazing out of my window up into the stars, expanding my horizons. I never did find that ring.

Desire is a bridge between what you want and the action required to get it. It is a wish and a longing. It is the art of discovery. When Galileo first discovered the three large moons of Jupiter, he knew there was at least one more, and his burning desire to know more was what kept the project going. It is the passion that burns inside to achieve a result, regardless of effort. It is a craving and a yearning to achieve something that you demand or expect. Yet the biggest lesson that I learned from that ring was that no matter how much desire I required, it never ran out. As long as I remained committed to the goal, the desire created an energy to take the action required—and to continue doing it.

This incident with the lost ring made my desire for everything stronger. It expanded my awareness tenfold. From that moment on, I knew that if I enacted desire, then whatever I wanted to achieve would be mine. So, I worked harder and more hours at my part-time job and made a pact to myself that I would commission myself a beautiful silver ring. One evening, about six years later, I realized that I had unconsciously created everything I wanted. I had made enough money in my part-time job to commission a ring, and I did just that. It was beautiful.

So, how exactly does one initiate desire? What does it take? For me, I think of my silver ring and where in the cosmos it has ended up, and I immediately get the feeling of desire, which inspires me into action. Steps that may be useful for you include:

Decide.

Empower yourself.

Standards: raise them.

Inspire: literally take a breath.

Respond to information and feedback.

Expand your horizons, look at it all from a new perspective.

My current desire is one of just as much significance as looking for the ring. We are currently in the throes of planning an empowerment event for 10,000 people! The desire is strong! I have made a **decision**. I have **empowered** myself and my team. We are currently raising our **standards** through trial and error and implementation of all positive learnings. We stop every now and then to **inspire** (breathe); this looks like team days and team holidays. We **respond** to information and feedback; our audience is very excited! And we are **expanding** daily to look at this project through the eyes of all the teams that will be involved. Desire is the fuel for every project we create; it is what keeps us going and going and going.

I wandered lonely as a cloud

That floats on high o'er vales and hills,

When all at once I saw a crowd,

A host, of golden daffodils;

Beside the lake, beneath the trees,

Fluttering and dancing in the breeze.

Continuous as the stars that shine

And twinkle on the Milky Way,

They stretched in never-ending line

Along the margin of a bay:

Ten thousand saw I at a glance,

Tossing their heads in sprightly dance.

The waves beside them danced; but they

Out-did the sparkling waves in glee:

A poet could not but be gay,

In such a jocund company:

I gazed—and gazed—but little thought

What wealth the show to me had brought:

For oft, when on my couch I lie

In vacant or in pensive mood,

They flash upon that inward eye

Which is the bliss of solitude;

And then my heart with pleasure fills,

And dances with the daffodils.

– *William Wordsworth (1802)*

ELIZABETH WALKER

About Elizabeth Walker: Elizabeth is Australia's leading Female Integrated NLP Trainer, an international speaker with Real Success, and the host of Success Resources's (Australia's largest and most successful events promoter, including speakers such as Tony Robbins and Sir Richard Branson) inaugural Australian Women's Program "The Seed." Elizabeth has guided many people to achieve complete personal breakthroughs and phenomenal personal and business growth. With over 25 years of experience transforming the lives of hundreds of thousands of people, Elizabeth's goal is to assist leaders to create the reality they choose to live, impacting millions on a global scale.

A thought leader who has worked alongside people like Gary Vaynerchuck, Kerwin Rae, Jeffery Slayter, and Kate Gray, Elizabeth has an outstanding method of delivering heart with business.

As a former lecturer in medicine at the University of Sydney and lecturer in nursing at W.tern Sydney University, Elizabeth was instrumental in the research and development of the stillbirth and neonatal death pathways, ensuring each family in Australia went home knowing what happened to their child, and felt understood, heard, and seen.

A former Australian Champion in Trampolining and Australian Dancesport, Elizabeth has always been passionate about the mindset and skills required to create the results you are seeking.

Author's website: *www.ElizabethAnneWalker.com*
Book Series Website & Author's Bio: *www.The13StepsToRiches.com*

Erin Ley

ENGAGE EVERY FIBER OF YOUR BEING

The definition of *desire*, for me, is the visceral feeling throughout my entire mind/body/spirit, whereby every fiber of my being is fully engaged, and solely focused on one goal.

When I was a little girl living in Brooklyn, my aunt, Rita McArdle, was one of the first female traders on Wall Street. She worked on the trading floor of Solomon Brothers located in downtown Manhattan. I was riding around Brooklyn and New York City in limousines with my aunt, and it felt amazing.

In 1973, when I was seven years old, she married Uncle Ed, and the New York Stock Exchange announced it on the ticker tape. Quickly thereafter, Aunt Rita and Uncle Ed went on to have the first of their three children, Meghan, whose birth was also announced on the New York Stock Exchange ticker tape. Soon after, Aunt Rita retired from Wall Street altogether.

I developed the burning *desire* to work on Wall Street. In 1988, I began to implement the vision I created and prepared for my entire life. Between 1988 and 1991, I worked for a few different brokerage houses, such as EF Hutton, Solomon Brothers, and Kidder Peabody. Aunt Rita helped me study for the Series 7 and Series 63 to become licensed.

"I don't need to study that much, Aunt Rita. I'm speaking 'bid' and 'ask' all day at work. I can calculate fractions in my sleep, and 'options' are easy."

"It's a difficult exam, Erin."

"Don't worry, Aunt Rita. I'm going out with my friends. See you tomorrow."

After standing in line for hours to enter the building, I spent another four hours on the exam. I was shocked at how difficult the questions were.

A few days later, I found out I failed. I developed the same burning *desire* to pass this exam that I had for working on Wall Street. I went to the Series 7 conferences, studied the material until I knew it in my sleep, and went back to take the exam a month later. I passed.

After becoming fully licensed, I went on to work as an account executive building my own accounts. I acquired the insurance license as well.

I did not realize how significant the character traits I developed over the years would prove to be at such a young age, until I was diagnosed with non-Hodgkins lymphoblastic lymphoma, a rare pediatric cancer that very few survived in 1991. I was twenty-five years old and drew from my seemingly never-ending depth of faith, tenacity, persistence, courage, confidence, and the visceral feeling throughout my entire mind/body/spirit, whereby every fiber of my being was engaged, solely focused on one goal, the burning *desire* to achieve whatever I put my mind to. Completely present. Completely focused. This was the time it mattered most. I had the white-hot burning *desire* to conquer cancer.

In March 1991, the symptoms began with a cough. Then, the cough deepened. I became dizzy. My gut told me to go to the ER.

"How old are you?" asked the physician in the ER.

"Twenty-five."

"Why are you wasting my time? I'm sure it's just stress," he continued.

"But I'm not stressed. The most stress I have right now is figuring out my weekend calendar," I said.

"Here's a prescription for Codeine," the doctor said, seemingly annoyed.

I didn't understand what was going on. I trusted the doctor because he donned the white coat, suggesting expertise. I filled the prescription and tried to figure out what was stressing me out.

In May 1991, I ended up back in the ER. This time, I could not breathe lying down. The same doctor with the hurry-up-and-get-out attitude greeted me at the entrance.

"You're back?" he asked.

"The symptoms are so much worse. Please do a chest x-ray."

"That's a complete waste of my time and yours," the doctor said, frustrated. "I bet my medical license there's nothing wrong with you."

I suddenly stepped way outside my comfort zone, made direct eye contact with the doctor, and told him I was not leaving the hospital until they did the x-ray. I jumped up on one of the hospital beds and told him I had all day.

The doctor ordered the x-ray. It took longer than usual as I sat there, waiting for the results.

"There's a shadow next to your heart. You have mitral-valve-prolapse. It's a very common condition for women. Here's the name and number of a cardiologist for you to see."

The doctor handed me a piece of paper and walked away.

A few days later, my breathing became even more problematic. I finally went to a pulmonologist. He sent me to the hospital for a CT scan. A few hours later, I ended up back in the ER, allergic to the CT scan dye.

As soon as my eyes met the eyes of the ER doctor with the hurry-up-and-get-out attitude, the fury I felt is indescribable.

"Stay the hell away from me! Did you cheat your way through med school? What's wrong with you? Stay away!" I screamed.

After many tests, such as chest needle biopsies and nuclear medicine scans, the results were in. The pulmonologist asked my parents to wait down the hall.

Alone in the room with him, he told me I had cancer.

I screamed a gut wrenching, "Noooooooooooo!" The time thereafter was a blur.

A friend of mine suggested a book titled, *Full Catastrophe Living*, by Jon Kabat-Zinn. In the back of the book, there was an order form for a mindfulness meditation cassette tape. This was the beginning of the biggest blessing of my life.

I had the white-hot burning *desire* to live. True health requires both a healthy body and a positive mind. Shakti Gawain's book titled *Creative Visualization* was another extremely important book I read at this time. It described how important visualizing exactly what I wanted was and the powerful effects it can have. I know this to be true based on the many miracles I continue to experience in my life.

In addition to Eckhart Tolle, Deepak Chopra, and many other personal development/self-help books I read, and cassette tapes I consumed, in 1991, I became obsessed with *Think and Grow Rich*, by Napoleon Hill. This book fascinated me and still does to this day. Like the human condition, this book goes deeper and deeper every time I read it.

I became ignited with the *desire* to THRIVE after cancer. I was determined to not only live, but to live my best life. I became my own biggest advocate, best friend, fully connected with God, and negated all doubt that I'd go on to live an extraordinary life.

Not only did I cheat death when the doctors told me I was going to die (a few times) during the two-and-a-half year protocol, when they told me that I would never have children after the protocol was over, I went on to have three healthy children without any medical intervention whatsoever.

My goals are always brought to life starting with the crystal-clear vision I create for myself, leading to my desired destiny. Napoleon Hill refers to it as a *Mission Statement*. I put pen to paper and write it all down, beyond my wildest dreams, in detail. My white-hot burning *desire* becomes the catalyst necessary to make my vision a reality. After bringing my vision alive utilizing the five senses, and sixth sense of intuition, maintaining the feeling as if my vision is happening right now, I then take massive action in the direction of my destiny, constantly defying the odds.

You too can create miracles in your life. I say that miracles are normal. When you know exactly what you want and you have the white-hot burning *desire* to achieve that definite goal, discounting all doubt, you'll become unstoppable.

The doctors at Memorial Sloan Kettering began to have their patients call me at home. They saw that I was able to do for myself, with the help of God, what they were unable to do. They saw me meditate, visualize, balance both hemispheres of the brain by listening to classical music and become incredibly intentional about guarding my thoughts carefully, staying focused on what was right with my life and everything I had to be grateful for. They saw me release negativity quickly. They saw me laugh more. They saw me go on to live my best life.

I'm blessed to be a contributing author in this extraordinary book series, based on the transformational book, *Think and Grow Rich*. All things are possible if you are open to the possibilities. Thank you, Erik Swanson, for the vision you've had for this book series, and the white-hot burning *desire* you've had to make it our reality!

ERIN LEY

About Erin Ley: As Founder and CEO of Onward Productions, Inc., Erin Ley has spent the last 30 years as an Author, Professional Speaker, Personal and Professional Empowerment and Success Coach predominantly around mindset, Vision and Decision. Founder of many influential summits, including "Life On Track," Erin is also the host of the upcoming online streaming TV show "Life On Track with Erin Ley," which is all about helping you get into the driver's seat of your own life.

They call Erin "The Miracle Maker!" As a cancer survivor at age 25, single mom of 3 at age 47, successful Entrepreneur at age 50, Erin has shown thousands upon thousands across the globe how to become victorious by being focused, fearless, and excited about life and your future! Erin says, "Celebrate life and you'll have a life worth celebrating!"

To see more about Erin and the release of her 4th book "*WorkLuv: A Love Story*" along with her "Life On Track" Course & Coaching Programs, please visit her website.

Author's website: *www.ErinLey.com*
Book Series Website & Author's Bio: *www.The13StepsToRiches.com*

Fatima Hurd

ASK AND YOU WILL RECEIVE

Life is driven by our desire for what we want in life. As a child, one of my biggest desires was to be successful. I realized that true success isn't reaching the destination, but instead, the experiences in between desire and achievement are what leads to our life purpose. My desire for success set me up for the right opportunities by following my intuition to achieve my desires.

When I was eighteen, I got a job in medical records. I had set the intention and desire that I was ready for something new and wanted to learn new skills.

A week earlier, I had gone in with my mom to see her podiatrist for her post-op check up. There we were, waiting, when Dr. Roberts walked in, who I must say had the best bedside manners. He asked my mom how she was feeling. He then turned to me and said, "Hello." He asked if I had any questions. I didn't, as he had covered any questions or concerns I did have during his conversation with my mom.

I knew I needed to approach him about a job before he left the room.

I asked, "Are you hiring by any chance?"

He said, "Yes, we have a medical record position that we need to fill."

He had me fill out an application at the front desk to be considered for the position.

I started there a week later. Before long, I had set a new goal of becoming a medical assistant for one of the doctors, which I later achieved.

I realize that when your desires are strong, you have a better chance of successfully achieving your goals, and as mentioned in the book *Three Feet from Gold*, you have to be committed, not just interested. That is how I found success with every job I held, because it was like a piece of the puzzle coming together to reveal my true life purpose. Every job that I had taught me new skills that were of much value for the next assignment.

Shortly after fulfilling my purpose as a medical assistant, it was time to move on to the next part of my life training. My desire led me to seek work in one of the resorts on the Las Vegas Strip. When I moved to Las Vegas from California in 1994, my first stop was the MGM, which was mesmerizing and majestic. My desire was strong, even at that young age. It set in motion to align the opportunities for the future that would eventually lead me to fulfill the intention I had set for myself at the moment.

I applied at the MGM and worked my way from one casino to the next and made it to Caesar's Palace. I remember being mesmerized by the beauty and the elegance of this casino. It was different; it had a prestige that no other casino had on the Strip, with all the extraordinary architecture that only Caesar's offers. I knew this was the place I desired to work. I made my way to the human resources office. I walked in and approached the lady who was behind the desk. I walked up and interrupted by tapping on the window in front of her desk.

She looked up at me with a smile and asked, "How can I help you?"

I said, "I am here to apply for the cage cashier position."

She said in a gentle voice, "I am sorry but that position was filled."

I was disappointed as I felt I had been guided there for a reason. I thanked her for her time as I turned around to walk away.

Just then, she stopped me and said, "I just got an email from the slot director. A change person position is available. Would you be interested?" she asked.

"Absolutely," I replied.

The following week, I went in for an interview, where I met with the managers. As one interviewed me, he asked, "Where do you see yourself in five years?"

I looked at him and said, "Sir, quite honestly, my desire is to be in a management position." Right there, I had set the intention for my desire to be in management.

I had the ambition and the desire to grow with the company. I was ready, so the opportunity showed up. I worked the night shift, and in the early hours of the morning, I ran into a nice lady. A week later at a meeting, she was presented as our new slot director. She later became my mentor and took me under her wing, and I learned a lot from her.

She had me sign up for a program offered by UNLV called Jumpstart Your Future for management. Caesars was bought by Harrah's, and I went to become a manager for that company at a different property. In 2008, during the recession, I was laid off, due to a staff reduction. I was devastated. Later, I realized my time there was over and that I had to move on. It was a blessing in disguise.

When I reflect back, I realized I had outgrown the position, and I needed something else to ignite my passion. However, my true purpose laid ahead, as my desire to become an entrepreneur got stronger.

One day at a meeting, I overheard a guy talking about a book called *Success Principles*, by Jack Canfield. I stopped at Barnes & Noble and picked up the book. I read the book and was hooked. I was ready to apply all the principles I had learned. This book was the first of many that led to my journey of self-improvement. It awakened my spirit and desire to become an entrepreneur. I never wanted to give anyone the power over me by telling me my worth. I felt empowered knowing that I was not being dependent on someone else for work. I was grateful for that chapter of my life, but it was time to move on.

I manifested an opportunity to become an entrepreneur when a friend approached me to go into business together and open a photography studio. After a couple of years, we parted ways. I opened my studio, Fatima Hurd Photography, which I ran successfully for many years until I moved from Las Vegas to California.

I took a break from starting my business all over again; I needed to earn income right away, so I got a job at the school district. I got a permanent position at a middle school, as a paraeducator. I was a one-on-one aid support for children with IEPs. The student I provided support for at the time had a class in the yearbook. I told the teacher about my background in photography, and she asked if I was willing to help teach the students how to use the cameras.

I was excited to teach the students how to use the cameras; however, my entrepreneurial spirit desired to launch my photography business. I pivoted my photography from portraiture to personal branding. I had a strong desire to get on Clubhouse, a new social media application. Little did I know that this was going to lead to many more great opportunities for self-improvement and collaboration.

One day, I was pinged into a room. As soon as I entered the room, I was invited on stage by Mr. Awesome! I wasn't sure why, but I agreed to it. At this point, I just knew to follow my intuition. I struggled with public speaking, and my desire was to improve, and once again, the Universe delivered. I was asked to give my pitch in sixty seconds and explain what collaboration meant to me. I spoke and was completely nervous. I can tell he sensed my struggle, but he was very kind. My desire to be better as a speaker brought this opportunity that led me to join his team, where I assist in the masterminds.

This opportunity led to an even bigger opportunity to fulfill another long-time desire that I had tucked away from my childhood and forgot about it until now. When I was young, I loved to write. My desire was to someday be an author. Even though it's been years, it is finally coming to fruition; I am one of the forty-six authors for this book.

I've spent my life connecting the dots, my desires, and all that I've manifested throughout my life. Desire was the foundation of the events that took place in my life that groomed me for the person I have become and will be in the future with a purpose. Without desire, there wouldn't be any goals to achieve, and life would be boring.

FATIMA HURD

About Fatima Hurd: Fatima is a personal brand photographer and was featured in the special edition of Beauty 8, Lifestyle's mommy magazine. Fatima specializes in personal branding photographs dedicated to helping influencers and entrepreneurs expand their reach online with strategic, creative, inspiring, and visual content. Owner of a digital consulting agency, Social Branding Digital Solutions, Fatima helps professionals with all their digital needs. Fatima holds years of photography experience. An expert in her field, she helps teach photography to middle school students and she hosts workshops to teach anyone who wants to learn how to use and improve their skills with DSLR and on manual mode. Hurd is also a mother of three, wife, certified Reiki master, a certified crystal healer. She loves being out in nature, enjoys talking to trips with her family, and loves meditation and yoga on the beach.

Author's website: *www.FatimaHurd.com*
Book Series Website & Author's Bio: *www.The13StepsToRiches.com*

Frankie Fegurgur

CREATE YOUR OWN LIFE

What if I told you that most of the desires you've had in your life weren't your own?

Think about your taste in music—where did it come from? Maybe you grew up hearing your mom playing her Beatles records. Then, one day, you met that rebel friend who was into The Misfits. I bet suddenly you plastered their poster on your wall, and even started dressing differently!

And then what happened? A few years ago, you heard Post Malone for the first time on Spotify, and you ran out to buy a pair of Crocs while screaming, "They said I would be nothing, now they always say congratulaaaaationnns!"

The influence of others in your choice of music is normal. But what about the rest of your life? Do you think it's healthy to live your life based on the subconscious behaviors of others? Especially when they don't even acknowledge their own desire?

In my contribution to this series, I'll discuss how the opinions of others will destroy your innate intelligence. But before I get too far ahead of myself, I'll share the story of how at the age of seventeen, I trusted my intuition over the opinion of my family, and never looked back.

I came home to an empty house one day after school. The logical thing would have been to do homework and enjoy the rare moment of quiet. However, something compelled me to walk half-a-mile to my friend's house.

I walked through their front door and looked to the right to see a United States Marine Corps recruiter sitting at the kitchen table. His uniform was crisp, and his presence filled the room. I wasn't sure what to do, so I sat down in the living room.

A few minutes later, I heard the words, "And what about him?" That's how I met the man who offered me the challenge of a lifetime. He made no promises, didn't tell me I was special, and accepted no compromises, only commitments.

I signed my enlistment contract even before my buddies. But there was a problem—my family expected me to go to college. I grew up in a family that worked hard, but lacked formal education. My grades were great, and I was decent enough in sports to receive a substantial offer from a private college.

Try as I might, I couldn't imagine sitting in a classroom for the first four years of adulthood. I craved earning my own money and seeing what the world had to offer. For me, the choice was clear; the only orientation that summer would be the thirteen-week bootcamp to become a Marine.

Eight weeks in, 9/11 happened. For anyone old enough to understand, we will never forget where we were that day. For me, it meant tough times were ahead.

Military service became synonymous with sacrifice. Sacrificing time away from family, sacrificing our physical and mental well-being, and even the loss of thousands of troops plus tens of thousands wounded. Even twenty years later, we are still a country at war.

And yet, serving was my greatest honor. Not for some politician's agenda, or corporate greed, but for the daily opportunity to look inside myself in a way that no classroom instruction could ever provide. I knew that I was willing to sacrifice everything—even my life—for the mission, especially if it meant the Marines on my left and right got to go home.

If you're wondering, yes, I still later became the first person in my family to graduate from college. Guess what got me into one of the most prestigious public universities in the world? Sharing my story of leading by example in a war 7,000 miles away from home.

Had I listened to the well-meaning words of those around me, we probably wouldn't be here today having this conversation. Fortunately, through my struggle, I developed a "burning desire" to continue to serve, this time for causes more in line with my higher purpose.

Notice I didn't say that I developed the "hobby" of volunteering, nor that occasionally I donated my spare change to the cause-of-the-day. I expected to live the life I desired and would accept no less.

To ensure we understand each other clearly, allow me to define desire in my own words. Desire is a reaction to an external thing that we begin to believe we need in our life. There are two types of desire: that of the ego and that of the elevated. Neither are wrong and should not be suppressed or controlled. That's because our desire provides important feedback on our state of mind, whether it's because we desire the thing to feel whole, or we come from a place of wholeness and seek purpose.

Desires of the ego start from a place of lacking. Imagine on your way home from work, you see a mansion. The mansion is amazing, and you just know that someone important lives there, maybe even a celebrity. Hours later, you continue holding the image of this mansion in your mind in stark contrast to your modest two-bedroom house. You bemoan the weeds in your yard, the outdated living room carpet, and how every time you flush the toilet, the person in the shower is startled by cold water. *If only I lived in that mansion,* you say to yourself.

You believe that if you had this thing, your life would be more exciting. You'd host lavish parties, and everyone would fight for an invitation. You'd be more attractive, and finally meet the spouse of your dreams. Unfortunately, odds are that even if you had this mansion, you'd still feel the lack. In fact, you may feel even more empty. You'd try again, this time with a fast car, or an exotic vacation, or an expensive bottle of alcohol.

And that's the thing with ego-driven desires. They are a craving that can be appeased relatively quickly, but will often lead to another inconsequential craving. It consumes you, leaving you further away from your ideal self.

An elevated desire is much different. It is the internal fire that burns brighter than any sun. It cannot be extinguished without your permission. Most likely, it can't be satiated by the attainment of a material thing. Only through the realization of a worthy goal will you finally rest, no matter how long it takes.

We must identify and harness our elevated desire to utilize the "Philosophy of Achievement." Only elevated desires will drive us through any obstacle, with nowhere to go but forward. With such a desire, you feel the future as if it has already been accomplished, leading you to act and behave accordingly. Once your identity catches up to your desire, the world falls in line. Just don't expect those who knew you before you embodied your desires to fall in line with them, too.

It's natural to be concerned with how your family and friends—and even perfect strangers—will perceive your journey. Remember, your desire and subsequent manifestation does not require their approval. Quite often, they don't believe in something until it's so real that it can't be denied—love them anyway.

Show empathy for your loved ones, because the hard truth is that they've probably given up on their fair share of desires. That's because most people quit before they ever really try. They give up, and blame the economy, or family obligations, but the truth is, they lacked clarity and *were never really committed in the first place.*

That's why becoming obsessively clear on your desire is so critical. I recommend you take a moment to tap into what I'm saying. Think back to a time where you wanted something so badly, it kept you up at night, and got you out of bed early in the morning. Something that didn't seem possible for you based on your circumstances, and yet, you found a way. You ignored warnings from friends and family, you learned new skills, and you even overcame your inner critic (or didn't even hear them at all)!

Maybe you've never had the courage to pursue something you desired, or never felt that rush of wanting something so badly that it made you dizzy. That might just be because someone lied to you about you being worthy—and until this point, you've believed them! This is YOUR journey, not your family's. Wish them well, and get back into the flow. You'll not only feel better, but you'll also instill elevated desires in others.

That's why I've written this chapter. My intention is to attract other leaders who are driven by their own burning desire to empower and serve, while lessening the suffering of those in need. My final question for you today is this: Is your leadership showing? If so, then I believe it makes sense for us to connect.

FRANKIE FEGURGUR

About Frankie Fegurgur: Frankie's "burning desire" is helping people retire with dignity. Frankie distills the lessons he has learned over the last 15 years and empowers our youth to make better financial decisions than the generation before them. This is a deeply personal mission for him—he was born to high-school-aged parents, and money was always a struggle. Frankie learned that hard work, alone, wasn't the key to financial freedom and sought a more fulfilling path. Now, he serves as the COO of a nonprofit financial association based in the San Francisco Bay Area, teaching money mindfulness. He, his wife, and their two children can be found exploring, volunteering, and building throughout their community.

Author's website: *www.FrankMoneyTalk.com*
Book Series Website & Author's Bio: *www.The13StepsToRiches.com*

Freeman Witherspoon

LET DESIRE BE YOUR LIGHT

I come from humble beginnings, and to me the finer things of life were just an illusion. A product of a small town in Alabama in the early sixties, I was raised by grandparents who could barely keep a roof over their heads. They took me into their home, along with two of my siblings and two of my cousins. Although times were hard, we always had food to eat and clean clothing, often hand-me-downs. Even during these trying times, I had a deep-seated desire to be a person of influence.

My grandmother was the family disciplinarian. She taught us right from wrong, the golden rule, and made sure we regularly attended church services. We all had daily chores, could play outside until dark, and had a set bedtime. These were the basics, and they were non-negotiable.

From an early age, I learned to work hard to earn my own money. My first job outside the home was gardening and yard maintenance for the elderly neighbors. The work was tedious and grueling under the Alabama sun, but it was quite refreshing being able to collect a few coins for my labor.

By the time I became a teenager, I knew there was another world on the other side of the tracks. I recall watching the freight train passing by and daydreaming of being carried away to some far-off land. All I could think about was getting away and making a better life for myself.

After graduation, I job-hopped around for a bit, searching for the proverbial golden ticket. My search led me to a career in the Army. Military service provided the discipline and other critical resources needed to realize some of my dreams. Now, with over twenty years of military service under my belt, a stable home, a family, and a steady income, you would think I would be content, but I was not.

I always dreamed of being a business owner. Although I know it takes just as much effort as working a nine to five, I am intrigued by the time freedom it brings. A few years prior to completing military service, I attended several entrepreneurial workshops. These workshops prepared me and opened my eyes to the realities of business. Growing up in the military, I didn't have much understanding of entrepreneurship. Advancing through military training and the business workshops gave me that mindset and the preparedness to make that dream come true.

Even though my dream didn't come to pass immediately, there is something that was birthed inside of me—desire. This is where I discovered that to achieve anything in life or to become anything, is all traceable to one thing, and that is desire. Desire is the anchor of all achievements. Gaining this understanding gave me that desire not to give up on my dreams.

What changed in me was that I knew that a healthy desire to advance in life is very important. I discovered throughout my military service that having a dream was not enough. What makes the dream a reality is the desire and the commitment. With desire growing into an obsession, it can provoke action to make the dream come true. This challenged me to set out in motion some of the businesses that are in place today. Even now, there are more unfolding business ideas that the desire has created within me.

Comparing and contrasting the stories of people who achieved greatness and stepped into their purposes irrespective of their ages made me know that it is never too late to make the dream I had within me come to pass. I knew that Charles Dickens had his desires come to pass. Thomas Edison also had his desires come to pass. Today, each one of us who can read at night or have the light glow in our rooms is blessed by Thomas Edison. It is the desire that he had that caused him to stay awake to make that a reality.

Growing up and not having a father or mother to look up to was painful. However, my grandparents did everything possible to make sure that we saw the best in life. Even though their efforts were meager, they created a vision that I can become something bigger and greater than what was revealed in my current circumstances. That created a deep desire in me, and that desire is what created me to be what I am today. Anything is possible in life when there is a desire.

A person with desire is always going to be successful. God has created the Universe or nature with laws and principles. Desire provokes the realities that cover nature to gravitate towards one who has desire. There are fortunes, treasures, wealth, and prosperity in this world. However, it is never going to come to manifestation until someone with desire takes action to convert the ideas to reality. Converting the ideas to reality provokes fortunes, blessings, and wealth from every part of the world towards you.

This is what Napoleon Hill, Henry Ford, Theodore Roosevelt, William Wrigley, John Wanamaker, Wilbur Wright, Thomas Edison, Andrew Carnegie, and many others did. They discovered the power of desire, and that desire unleashed the inherent power, wealth, and treasures that were within them. This makes us marvel and then see the wonder of desire. Desire can provoke even healing, deliverance, and the restoration of one's health.

Personally, understanding this outstanding concept and principle set me on the road to financial freedom. It challenged me to become a person of purpose and discipline as well. Even though at the beginning of my life, I didn't get things easy, as I grew up, things changed. That change; however, just didn't bring me everything I needed in life. I needed peace, love, and happiness. I didn't get all of these. I knew there was something that was missing in me. This set me out on a quest—a quest to find answers. It was there I discovered that life is going to be a mystery until one discovers their purpose. Purpose embodies all the mysteries of wealth, treasures, joy, peace, and happiness in life. That opened my eyes and changed the way I viewed myself and the world around me.

In the pursuit of my entrepreneurial dreams, a turning point eventually happened in my health. I had that point or moment where I was sick and couldn't work. I had a spinal issue that kept me bedridden for months. During those times, I had something to be hopeful for. Even though it looked like everything was falling apart, there was some kind of energy and faith within me that challenged me to be hopeful. This energy and vibration changed everything around me. Amid that dilemma, I also decided to use that time to fellowship with God. I restored my relationship with God in that darkness. Trust me, that became my therapy. God began to open my eyes to the realities of my purpose and destiny, and He showed me the way to live and be a man in that "Valley."

After that experience, I understood a principle that is an integral part of life. That time of stillness gave me the ability to see beyond myself. It also gave me insight into my life's purpose. What I am today is a function of that encounter. Then, I discovered the incredible power of desire. Nothing in this world changes until there is a desire to change it. Nothing can see transformation until there is a desire to make that happen.

Desire is like a magnet; it can attract anything in life. That means we can attract healing, money, fame, fortunes, and wealth with it. So, use your desire well, and you will see the power of it. After all of these experiences and the increase that desire has brought me, I can recommend that if you have a desire, you can do incredible things. If you can dare have the desire to prosper, you can prosper. If you dare have a desire to be healthy and well, you are going to become healthy and well. If you dare have the desire to change things in and around you, then that can happen. Whatever you desire, that is exactly what nature is going to bring to you. The moment there is a desire to make something happen, you have created room to unleash the inherent abilities in that thing.

In conclusion, desire can be grown. It is like a seed, and you can make it grow with nourishment and care. As you keep focusing on your desires, those desires will mature and eventually become an obsession. When it gets to that level, it takes you to the place of action. The action gets the job done. Desire takes you to the job; whereas, actions push the job to happen. In addition, each one of us must befriend desire, and then we can see tremendous changes in our lives.

FREEMAN WITHERSPOON

About Freeman Witherspoon: Freeman is a professional network marketer that manages several online businesses. He considers himself a late bloomer to network marketing. Prior to partnering with network marketing organizations, he served for over 20 years in the military. He has incorporated his many life experiences into managing successful business models.

Military service afforded him the opportunity to travel throughout the world. He has lived in Heidelberg, Germany, Seoul, South Korea, and many places throughout the United States. Freeman currently lives in Texas with his wife and three dogs: a Dachshund named Dutchess, a Yorkie named Boosie and a Pomchi (Pomeranian-Chihuahua mix) named Caesar.

Author's website: *www.FWitherspoonJr.com*
Book Series Website & Author's Bio: *www.The13StepsToRiches.com*

Gina & Jay Bacalski

MY MOON

What is your Fairytale? For me, England was my moon. You know, the moon, that impossible dream that you don't think you'll ever get to achieve, so you may as well ask for it instead? I was six, I had just learned to read, and I was pouring over classic fairytales; At least the ones about true love and pretty dresses and kissing. In my understanding, at the time, every fairytale happened in England. Cinderella, Robin Hood, Sleeping Beauty all resided somewhere in that enchanted land. England still had princesses, after all: Princess Diana. And she was just as lovely and had just as pretty dresses as the princesses in my books. Oh, how I longed to go to England, to see all the magic happening! I can still feel my little six-year-old body positively aching with the desire to be there.

Of course, I knew that could never happen. No one ever left Enoch, Utah. You grew up there, graduated high school, and then you got married, had babies, and then you died. Everyone knew that's what happened. No one ever left; we couldn't afford to. Especially not to places like England and especially not for people like me.

Homeschooled till sixth grade, the only social interaction I had with peers was at church. My family of nine had pulled the single wide manufactured home off the lot from the trailer park and set it up on two newly acquired farm acres in the county, where dirt roads and jackrabbits were abundant. A makeshift lean-to and shed quickly erected, and farm animals soon inhabited the once empty sage-brush-scattered field.

I distinctly recall my first Sunday at church sitting in Sunday School. I was in my older sister's outgrown dress. It was a little faded, but it was clean, and my hair brushed. My teacher, hoping to instill an object lesson, asked: "What are houses made out of?" The girl to my left said her house was made of bricks. The boy to the right said his was made of wood. I raised my hand and said that mine was made out of aluminum. Everyone laughed. I stopped answering questions.

Being underprivileged and relatively friendless didn't stop me sucking up every bit of pre-internet data about England as I could. I even developed an immaculate British accent! I vividly remember when *Robin Hood Prince of Thieves* starring Kevin Costner came out. I must have watched it at least 23 times. You see, Robin Hood was my boyfriend. The animated Disney Robin Hood as a fox had been a long-time sweetheart of mine and had rescued me from the villainous King John countless times in play and daydreams.

In high school, my discovery of Jane Austen fueled my longing for a place I had never been. I devoured all things Austen and even threw in some Dickens and Bronte sisters. England had never been more seductive.

When I graduated high school, I had one goal: To move far away! And I did so with the help of a nanny agency. I moved to Boston,

MA. There I became the nanny to an affluent and incredibly generous family with two young girls. Little did I know how that one choice would shape my future.

While in Boston, England purred at me in the most unexpected ways. My nanny family hosted a soccer coach (or futbol as they call it) in an exchange program from London. Steve and I became fast friends, and we quickly developed a big brother, little sister relationship. He asked me all about America, and I pestered him with questions about England. I couldn't help but think, was this a sign?

It was also in Boston that I discovered the magical world of Harry Potter. I quickly devoured every book and movie many times over.

One night, I was talking on the phone with another friend, a Boston local. While discussing plans of what I should do when my nanny family was away on their annual two-week sailing trip, I shared with him my burning desire to go to England. "Well, why don't you go?" he asked, "it's just a small hop across the pond."

That was the first time I heard the Atlantic Ocean referred to as "the pond." A pond? I knew what a pond was, we used them for irrigation back home. They were pretty small. Was England that close?

I sat in stunned silence for all of five seconds, but for me it was five eternities. All space and time had stopped. My head and fingers started physically buzzing and my vision blurred. My mind churned with thoughts, possibilities, and unanswered questions. Could I actually go to my England? But I was a county dweller from Enoch Utah. We didn't achieve dreams there, those were always squashed by survival.

But England isn't so far away; what was stopping me? Why exactly couldn't I go? Being a pampered New England Nanny, I had more than enough means. My chest heaved as my breathing intensified, and I saw six-year-old Gina sitting in the middle of that small patch of worn carpet; Cinderella opened on her lap. Was England something we could touch? "Well, why don't you go? It's just a small hop across the pond" my Fairy-Godmother-friend's words echoed across my mind.

And then something happened I never intended, but just like Cinderella to her fairy Godmother, I would be forever grateful for. In those five eternal seconds, going to England was no longer an impossible dream or far distant fantasy. For the first time, it became a *choice*.

That night, I bought the first-class standby plane tickets my fairy godmother offered. Two weeks later, I packed a single backpack, my best friend Kassie, and got on an airplane.

Even though the large "Mind the Gap" sign made me chuckle, and the thick fog that blanketed the countryside and made it almost impossible to drive in were all signs that I wasn't in Boston anymore, being in England didn't seem real to me until I arrived at the exact place my heart had yearned for so badly.

On the wrong side of the road, on the wrong side of the newly hired car, I remember driving on a "motorway" along Hadrian's Wall in Northern England, determined to find the tree and the spot. When I would stop and ask for directions, I would always get the same "Oh bout three o' fo miles, dat-away," and a vague hand waggle to the west. Until, at long last, there it was.

Jet lagged and bleary-eyed, I nearly floated the short distance from the car park to the great tree. A tree that up until that moment I had only seen in the opening scenes of Robin Hood Prince of Thieves, where my daring beloved rescued a boy who had taken shelter from the vile soldiers of the Sheriff of Nottingham!

There I stood, on the same ancient wall as my childhood love, and looked out across the endless swaths of emerald before me, tears making salty trails down my cheeks.

I had done it. I brought myself there. I was Cinderella and my own Prince Charming. I felt so complete, accomplished, utterly fulfilled. I reached for the stars, and here they were, glittering in my hands, filling my heart to overflowing. I profusely thanked my Father in Heaven for the moment, the beauty surrounding me, and the dream realized.

I then did the only thing that seemed logical.

I hugged my tree; I smelt the grass, I lay on the wall, hungrily running my fingers across all within my reach.

Not to let any of my senses escape, I had even stuck out my tongue and let it trace patterns on the wall as I closed my eyes and let that moment soak in my heart for eternity.

To this day, over fifteen years later, I can hear the gentle winds rustle the leaves of my tree and tickle the long grass before it caresses my face and plays with my hair. I smell the damp, clean earth. I taste the minerals and salt and grit of the stones that make up the wall. I see the vast, jade quilt before me.

You know that moment, where you finally get what you've longed for, and then you realize that it wasn't that great after all? Well, that moment never came. I will always be homesick for England!

So I'll ask again, what's your fairytale? Are you like I was, stuck in all the impossibilities that you can't see the pumpkin carriage in front of you? To some people, what I did may have seemed like no big deal. But for a poor, small girl from nowhere, where people did nothing, I now proudly wear the moon on a chain around my neck. Who knew all I needed to do, was to reach out and take it!

~Gina Bacalski

GINA & JAY BACALSKI

About Gina Bacalski: Gina is a Real Estate Agent, licensed since June 2018. Her background is in Early Childhood Education where she received her Child Development Associate from the state of Utah and has an AS from BYU-Idaho. For the past 17 years, Gina thoroughly enjoyed her experience in the service industry helping families in the gifted community.

In 2019, Gina helped Jon Kovach Jr. launch Champion Circle and is now CEO of the organization. She brings her genuine love for people, high attention to detail, and strives to exceed client's expectations to the Real Estate industry and to Champion Circle.

Gina married the man of her dreams, Jay Bacalski, in San Diego, in 2013. The Bacalski's love entertaining friends and family, going on hikes, and attending movies and plays. When Gina isn't helping her clients navigate the real estate world, she will most often be found dancing and listening to BTS, watching KDramas and writing fantasy, sci-fi and romance novels.

Author's website: *www.facebook.com/ginahintz*
Book Series Website & Author's Bio: *www.The13StepsToRiches.com*

Griselda Beck

GIVE YOURSELF CHOICES

Desire: the passion, the burning compulsion to have or experience something or someone. Another way to look at this is vision, intention, and motivation—wanting something so much that you would be and do anything to make it happen.

Have you ever wanted something so badly that all you could do was think about it? So often, we get stuck here, because we begin to imagine what it will look like... AND we confuse desire with the image we have created in our minds.

As a motivational speaker and business coach for entrepreneurs, I always begin the journey with a new client by asking what it is they want. Usually, it's something along the lines of getting their first client, breaking through six figures, or creating freedom of time and flexibility in their business, so they can enjoy the life they live. I invite my clients to take it a step further and find out WHY they want what they want. Their response is usually something along the lines of wanting to have fun again, experience fulfillment, joy, love, freedom, relaxation, deeper connections, less stress, family, experience adventure, travel, etc.

I love when they discover their core WHY, as this reveals their CORE DESIRE! This gets to be the beacon that will guide us over the next 12 months and beyond. Too often, the problem isn't that they are doing things wrong, but rather, a matter of doing the right things that move them towards fulfilment of this core desire. This, my friends, is a matter of heart, authenticity, and our true self. I know this as on my own journey, I lost sight of what my core desire was. Here's a part of my story:

In my early thirties, I became everything I had dreamed of as a young woman. I was the youngest and only female minority executive of a multi-million-dollar public company. I owned my home, traveled extensively, and pretty much "had it made." I had arrived... but I wasn't happy. I thought I was pursuing my core desire of being in such power, responsibility and I thought happiness. Along the way, I did whatever it took to get there—worked an insane number of hours, missed out on important events for those closest to me, created distance between myself and others, stating they "just didn't understand," and my health took a dive, too. So much so that one day, I experienced a medical emergency that brought my life to a screeching halt.

I had accomplished everything I had set out to do; I was a corporate executive within seven years of completing my MBA. I did everything right! AND... I wasn't doing the right things. I didn't take it one step further to understand WHY I wanted those things in the first place. In my mind, that position and status equated to freedom, time, and money, which would enable me to travel leisurely any time I wanted, enjoy life, have fun, and be happy. Well... what I created was far from that reality. My TRUE CORE DESIRE was to feel FREE! What I created was a trap. I was successful, nonetheless, but the lifestyle I was living, constantly on-the-go, sustained by caffeine and adrenaline, was not sustainable long-term.

Fast forward to today: I now ensure my clients are very clear on their core desire, because true success is achieved when you get to experience it at every step in your journey. I have built a coaching practice around empowering others to create a life that you don't need a vacation from. My clients create habits and dedicate space on their calendars that create the experience they truly desire.

My core desire is freedom. I have learned over time this means creating choice in my life. I get to choose how I spend my time. I've built a career that feels like a total dream life and privilege to have. I feel incredibly energized immediately following a coaching session or after delivering a keynote speech. You know that feeling many describe as "runner's high"? I experience that for hours! It doesn't feel like "work." So much so that I still get to be very mindful of my time as a whole, because when you love something this much, it is easy to invest all of yourself in it and quickly end up in a workaholic state again. By the way, the same is true in relationships... people can get "lost" in their significant others, their kiddos, their hobby, etc.

Humans are multidimensional beings. It is important that we are fulfilling our core desire in every aspect of our life—professional, social, family, relationships, financial, spiritual, physical, and mental. For me, that means I get to create a life where I feel FREE in each of those areas. Looking back now, it is easy to see how I wasn't happy having "had it all," as my definition of "having it all" was primarily centered around professional growth and financial stability. Working ninety hours a week didn't allow much time to focus on the other aspects of my life. They existed, but they were nowhere near a score of 10/10. More like a 6/10, and who wants to settle for a D in life!

So, where did I get off track? And how did I get back on track? Glad you asked!

As a child, I was obsessed with puzzles! There was GREAT satisfaction in completing the puzzle... not so much the process; I lived for the final moment of connecting the last piece! Addicted to that feeling, I learned to be maniacally committed to crossing the finish line and "problem solving" everything! (P.S. My romantic partners have not appreciated this skill as much as corporate America. Hard lesson, which I'll share another time.) This served me very well in life otherwise. I learned that I could accomplish anything I set my mind to that I truly DESIRED!

As a teenager, I lit up when I was entrusted with great responsibility. I felt a sense of importance and achievement, and thus, began to align my desires to things that would give me this feeling. At some point, the lines became blurred, and I wanted what I experienced and understood success to be: making a lot of money and a big, important job means you can do anything you want!

As I graduated college and made my way into the corporate world, my puzzles became the company with all of its complex pieces—resources, people, clients, objectives, etc. I chose behaviors and actions that aligned with creating extraordinary results in terms of solving problems, earning a bigger paycheck, and increasing responsibility. I felt important. It gave me the freedom I longed for. I could buy anything I wanted, travel where I wanted, and for a long time, LIFE WAS GOOD... for a time. As I continued to pursue greater success, I began to trade in joy, self-care, and fun for working more. As if working more was eventually going to bring more freedom... more happiness. I was chasing more of what I thought I wanted, "success - title and money," versus more of what I truly desired: freedom.

I want you to know what I have come to learn: both can be true; you can create happiness and a highly successful career. The secret lies in these daily practices I have now incorporated into my routine and recommend to my clients and any audience I'm speaking to:

1. What am I grateful for today?

2. What do I want?

    a. What do I want to experience?

    b. What do I want to feel?

3. I rate my day on a scale of 1-10 at the end of each day and ask, what was in the gap?

4. What am I committed to creating tomorrow?

If you don't know where to start, ask yourself: if money was no object and you had no one else but yourself to think about, what would your life look like? Giving yourself permission to think this way, removing all circumstances, is a great first step to identifying your vision... authentically... then take it one step further and ask yourself: why? What would you want to experience? Lastly, what is one step you can take right now to move you towards that vision?

This brings me to my final thoughts, the wisdom I live by now, the advice I would give my younger self: ALWAYS STAY CURIOUS! When we do this work once and don't revisit it periodically, we become automatic, like Ronco's Showtime "Set it and forget it!" Our life is on autopilot or we leave things out because "that's just the way it is," which leads us to unfulfillment at the exact point in which we surpass the fulfillment of that path. Life is a journey with many different paths and infinite possibilities available to us. Choose the path that aligns to your core desire! Never settle for less than 10/10! In every moment, you get to choose.

GRISELDA BECK

About Griselda Beck: Griselda Beck, M.B.A. is a powerhouse motivational speaker and coach who combines her executive expertise with transformational leadership, mindset, life coaching, and heart-centered divine feminine energy principles. Griselda empowers women across the globe to step into their power, authenticity, hearts, and sensuality, to create incredible success in their business and freedom in their lives. She creates confident CEOs.

Griselda's clients have experienced success in quitting their 9-5 jobs, tripling their rates, getting their first client, launching their first product, and growing their business in a way that allows them to live the lifestyle and freedom they want. She has been featured as a top expert on FOX, ABC, NBC, CBS, MarketWatch, Telemundo, and named on the Top 10 Business Coaches list by Disrupt Magazine.

Griselda is an executive with over 15 years of corporate experience, founder of Latina Boss Coach and Beck Consulting Group, and serves as president for the nonprofit organization MANA de North County San Diego. She also volunteers her time teaching empowerment mindset at her local homeless shelter, Operation Hope-North County.

Author's website: *www.LatinaBossCoach.com*
Book Series Website & Author's Bio: *www.The13StepsToRiches.com*

Jason Curtis

ON BEING GENUINE AND KIND

When you have a burning desire, there is nothing stopping you from whatever you want in life. You have to make sure you have a clear picture and look at it and feel the emotions you would have if you were already there. Visualize several times a day to ingrain it into your head.

This principle is not about passion, nor motivation; it is solely about that burning desire for what you really want. Any obstacle which comes your way will be just that, a small obstacle along the way!

Every day, I have this burning desire to be a better person. I've had many experiences in my life that have taught me this. From beating childhood cancer to enlisting in the Navy, marrying my wife, and starting a family, I desire to make the greatest choices that make the greatest impact in my life each day.

I understand that choosing to be a better person each day is a habit, just like desire is a major habitude (habit and attitude) and step to riches. The best daily habit for my burning desire is to wake up and focus on being grateful and present—do not take any minute of the day or experience for granted. Everything happens for a reason! This habit drives my personal success year after year.

Knowing what I know now, the greatest advice I can give to my younger self is to live in the moment of now. Find a lesson to learn in every circumstance that crosses your path. Have that burning desire to be a better person. These are the principles that, if applied, create lifetimes of happiness.

My reading and life experiences have taught me some very valuable techniques and strategies in applying and maintaining a burning desire:

1. Fix exactly what you want.

2. Determine the correct path.

3. Establish a fixed date.

4. Create a path and ACT!

5. Delay gratification and a clear statement of what you exchange in this pursuit.

6. Read this statement in the morning and evening.

In the last five years, the mentor with the most impact on me has been Tim Jarvinen, co-founder and co-owner of Bonvera, also an all-star football and basketball athlete, and a Delphi automotive engineer. Through his mentorship and support, he has spent a great deal of his time sharing his intense desire for me to show and share my heart with others and to be genuine in every interaction I have. Based on that principle of being genuine with others, I've learned to create relationships based on love and respect. I have a burning desire to build those relationships throughout my life.

On this journey of success, while utilizing the desire as a major step to riches, what has surprised me the most is that I've been more genuine and loving in my interactions. In creating genuine relationships of love and respect, I've gained more than I could ever dream of! This principle isn't exclusive to just my life—anyone can utilize it and obtain similar results or even better ones.

I've found that my best strategy to overcome adversity and obstacles is to realize that I have two daughters who are always watching me do the right things. My burning desire to be genuine in my word as well as my actions have awarded me the luxuries of being a stalwart example of a father and a hero to them. Also, if you are genuine and caring when you interact with others and provide a solution to a need of your clients, then you will be successful in whatever you are doing and pursuing.

Be honest and ethical, have integrity, genuinely love your fellow men and women, and be the best version of yourself are some of the most powerful age-old habits used to overcome adversity and obstacles. These habits are the driving force for desire.

Being an entrepreneur is all about running YOUR own marathon. It isn't a sprint! Align yourself with the right people with similar burning desires and you will find a much more fulfilled life. Life isn't all about riches, and your core values will help you attract the communities that help you stay the course.

Set your days up for ultimate success and maximum impact by having a burning desire within you to always do the right thing. Having a desire to help others, without assuming any other gain, I have chosen to make each moment about the people I spend time with and to be as positive and uplifting as I can. It's a burning desire that anyone can have, obtain, and even maintain to ultimately reach the riches you so dream about.

JASON CURTIS

About Jason Curits: Jason has been a serial entrepreneur for 15 years and has enjoyed serving and helping his fellow entrepreneurs build their businesses and win in this game of life-on purpose! Jason created On Purpose Coaching because he knew, through his life experiences, that he could create an impact in others. He focuses on helping his clients create better relationships with their customers. This fosters trust and rapport while generating customer loyalty.

Jason is a Navy Veteran of six years. He has sailed the seas and oceans in serving his God and country. Curtis and his wife, Brianna, have been married for eight years, and they have two children.

Author's website: *www.OnPurposeCoaching.com*
Book Series Website & Author's Bio: *www.The13StepsToRiches.com*

Jeffrey Levine

EVERYTHING IS OPEN TO YOU WHEN YOU HAVE STRONG ENOUGH DESIRE

The Spark of Desire Is Generally Event-Driven

I grew up in a family where I heard the word "no" a lot. There was a reason for the answer, which was generally that we couldn't afford it. Overall, I got used to hearing "no," and it wasn't a big deal—until a trip to the dentist when I was a teenager.

As a teenager, I experienced excruciating jaw pain. Every day when I awoke, I felt the pain. It grew worse and worse, inciting me to eventually tell my parents about it. They suggested we make an appointment with our dentist. Thankfully, he told us that he had a solution for my problem, a way to eliminate my jaw pain: I needed to wear a retainer at night. I was thrilled! But when he shared with my parents how much the retainer would cost, that same old answer reared its ugly head: "No." We couldn't afford it.

I was shocked. I was distraught. And I was extremely upset that this simple solution was out of my reach. Instead of getting the retainer, I was going to have to live in pain. But that wasn't the world in which I wanted to live. I vowed right then that I would never let this happen to me again.

Because of that situation, I had a *burning desire* to be successful and create abundance in my life.

With Desire, Doors Open

Our neighbor, an attorney, invited me to join him in court. I relied on my standby response. I said, "No." Eventually, though, I tried a new answer: "Yes."

Because of my earlier experiences, I had cultivated a burning desire to be financially successful in life and never suffer again. After joining my neighbor in court and seeing his smiling clients pay him with crisp hundred-dollar bills, I thought, *This is for me!* When I graduated college, my neighbor helped me get into law school. And once I was there, my burning desire was alight.

My goal in law school was to do so well that I would be able to land a really good job. Since I was one of the best students, my tax professor recommended I take an extra year of law school to focus on taxation. He offered to write me a recommendation and told me that extra focus year would provide me with a specialty career path.

After finishing law school with my taxation specialty, I was offered a great job with a national tax and financial planning firm. This position allowed me to learn so much while I was making good money. There, I was able to work with top executives and successful business owners. And that led to me starting my own business. Unfortunately, since I didn't know anything about marketing, it took a long time for my business to start making money. Plus, without a mentor to lead the way, I made mistake after mistake in my business operations.

What I did do, though, was start to create interest. I wrote a column for a local business paper, appeared on radio and TV shows, and was interviewed in national financial publications. Slowly, things started to change. More people knew about me and wanted to do business with me. Once I helped a client with a complex IRS audit and took another business owner's firm public, my business began growing even faster. Eventually, I had my own radio show every Monday night for many years and did TV segments in the morning and night.

Because of this exposure and getting referrals from existing clients, I started making good money. And that meant, years after the dentist first diagnosed my condition, I could afford that retainer. When I visited the dentist and he told me the price, I didn't hesitate. I said "yes" to no more pain.

Deep Desire Leads to Deep Results

During one of my regular gym workouts, I was approached by a woman who said that she and her partners were interested in buying my business. She asked if I was available the following day to meet with them and discuss the deal. Following my desire for success, I once again didn't hesitate. I responded with an emphatic, "Yes." That next day, we had a deal.

Shortly thereafter, I moved from New York to Arizona to enjoy a life of sunshine and beauty. In my retirement, I played golf every day.

I thought that would make me happy; however, after a few years, I found that I was bored with this new life. I needed something else.

When attending a conference with a friend, I had the opportunity to listen to a compelling keynote speaker. What he shared really resonated with me, and I had a burning desire to meet and get to know him. I secured his contact information and called him. We spoke about potentially getting on stage together, which became a reality before too long.

This new friend reached out to me before the end of the year and asked me to fly to California to be in a documentary. Again, without hesitation, I responded, "Yes." It was an exhilarating and challenging experience, and I learned a lot about doing documentaries. It made me want to do more of them. After participating in five documentaries, I knew I was ready for the big time.

I was invited to be the executive producer of and cast member in the documentary *Beyond the Secret: The Awakening*. What a great experience! I made new friends and was seen on Amazon Prime. The documentary has even received twelve national and international awards.

But even with that amazing experience, I had a burning desire to return to the world of financial planning. I started attending seminars where I met meeting planners. Unfortunately, this was during the COVID-19 pandemic, and no one was hiring.

Unexpectedly, I received a call from a financial planner I had met previously. She was interested in having me join her firm. I decided to get back in the business. It had been a number of years since I'd worked in financial planning, so I embarked on a journey to learn as much as possible during the downtime of the pandemic. I spent four to six hours every day learning everything I could. Because of COVID-19, the trainings were held virtually, via Zoom, which enabled me to catch up and be ready to help clients.

Once back in the financial planning world, I decided to focus my practice on helping business owners exit their businesses rich. I developed the "second 40" concept, meaning that during the first sixty years of life, you accumulate as much money as you can to retire, and then the next forty years, you discover new opportunities to live a meaningful life in which you can have a positive impact and learn the latest about health and vitality.

I am just embarking on this experience, and it's very exciting, since it is what I was doing in my career before I sold my company. Going through it all, I realized that my burning desire is what got me to this place. It all started when I was a teenager and was denied the opportunity to end my jaw pain with a retainer. That sparked my burning desire.

You can have the same burning desire that drives your life and leads you to unimaginable success.

Making the Most of Your Burning Desire

Every person has something in them that they would love to do, but unfortunately, they often don't give themselves permission to pursue their dreams. When you decide what you really want, you'll create a burning desire to get it. And that desire is what will help you to push through the challenges that feel uncomfortable along the way.

Fear is an emotion that will run right up against your desires. It can be a massive fear, a "terror barrier." We've learned not to go there, not to embrace discomfort. Instead of facing that barrier, we fall back on what we've always been taught: *I'm not good enough; I can't; why me?* These paradigms are here to keep us safe, and if you listen to them, you will, indeed, stay safe. But you won't realize your burning desire.

The paradigm shifts when you get really clear about what you want. You then realize that your terror barriers and paradigms are pulling you back from what you desire. You need to have a burning desire so deep that it will break through fear. Just as Spanish conquistador Hernán Cortés told his men to burn the boats so they could not turn back when they reached the New World, you have to have the same attitude when it comes to your goals. Failure is not an option. You can be so amazing when there's no other option but to push through.

Remember that when you have a burning desire and a commitment, you don't have to worry about the "how." The how will show up. The Universe is abundant when you have a clear intention and direction. You have to stop talking about "someday," because that is not a day on the calendar. The only day is today. When you make a decision and commit to it, everything you need will show up.

Make your choice, make that desire palpable, and burn the ships. Then, everything you ever imagined you could achieve will be available for you.

JEFFREY LEVINE

About Jeffrey Levine: Jeffrey is a highly skilled tax planner and business strategist, as well as a published author and sought-after speaker. He's been featured in national magazines, on the cover of *Influential People Magazine,* and is a frequent featured expert on radio, talk shows, and documentaries. Jeffrey attended the prestigious Alba Academy for high school and then went on to University of Hartford at Connecticut, University of Mississippi Law School, Boston University School of Law, and earned an L.L.M. in taxation. His accolades include features in *Kiplinger* and *Family Circle Magazine,* as well as a dedicated commentator for Charmel 6 and 13 news shows, a contributor for the *Albany Business Review,* and an announcer for WGY Radio.

Jeffrey has accumulated more than 30 years of experience as a tax attorney and certified financial planner and has given in excess of 500 speeches internationally. Levine is the executive producer and cast member in the documentary *Beyond the Secret: The Awakening.*

Jeffrey's most current work, *Consistent Profitable Growth Map, is* a step-by-step workbook outlining easy-to-follow steps to convert consistent revenue growth to a business platform.

Author's website: *www.JeffreyLevine.Solutions*
Book Series Website & Author's Bio: *www.The13StepsToRiches.com*

Lacey and Adam Platt

MOVING HEAVEN AND EARTH & ASK FOR WHAT YOU WANT

Moving Heaven And Earth

Desire is more than simply wanting. It's every fiber of your being, every cell in your body, every nerve ending and sense that runs from the top of your head to the tips of your toes wanting "it," whatever "it" may be.

Imagine I am holding a piece of chocolate under your nose. You can smell its sweet aroma. You open your mouth and place this morsel of goodness on your tongue, and now, you can taste the sweetness and feel its velvety smoothness. Your mouth starts to fill with saliva as the chocolate begins to melt into a puddle on your tongue, and as you swallow, the chocolate slides down the back of your throat thinly coating as it glides into your tummy. Now, every part of you wants that chocolate, doesn't it?

My definition of the word desire means, "I MUST have that in my life, and I am willing to do whatever it takes." When I was a kid, my mom would say, "I would move Heaven and Earth for that." Now, when I think of that, I think, *Heaven and Earth? Well, that's pretty much everything!* So, if I were going to move everything to get this thing, I would say, "I would move Heaven and Earth to get it." I feel it with every single cell in my body, from the tip of my toes, all the way to the top of my head. That, my friend, is DESIRE.

So, let's first figure out what you really want. Ask yourself, *What do I want?* Pull out a piece of paper; let's activate your brain. This allows you to get it all out of your brain and look at it. So, if you're thinking, *I want chocolate. I want a new job. I want _____* (whatever it is that you want), write it down, no matter how silly it seems. If I say, *I want a piece of chocolate*, that means, *Lacey, go get a freaking piece of chocolate.* It doesn't mean that it was silly or stupid or that I shouldn't write it down. It's just not the big picture or the big goal of what I really want. What we're looking for here is that overall thing that you want.

You say, "I want a car." Great! A car is part of it. Let's think bigger. "I want a house." Okay. What kind of house? Let's talk about how this house looks. How does this car feel when you drive it? Sometimes, people will get a new house or car, and they still don't feel complete. They'll still feel like they want something, that's because it's usually more of a lifestyle. It's more than just one thing, and it really encompasses all aspects of your life. Some say, "I want a new job," and I say, "Okay, what will a new job allow you to do?" What is it that you really want?

Most of the time, people are very superficial, thinking, *I want a house or a new job.* But when you can get them to look deeper, what they really want is freedom. Freedom to have the money to buy a new house, a new car, or work a job they enjoy. The meaning becomes so much deeper. What they really were looking for all this time was going into business for themselves. They get to work the hours they want and get the pay that they want. They can travel, buy the house, car, boat, whatever. The deeper want is a lifestyle, not the superficial house or car. Those things come with that lifestyle, and that's what I'm trying to get people to see.

When you do this activity, really figure out what it all leads towards. What does it look like? The more precise, the better. When you close your eyes and visualize this, have all the details in place.

That's what I'm looking for as an achievement coach. I want you to achieve that deep, fulfilling want. When I can get you to start working towards that, you'll start seeing the steps. Visualization becomes belief. All those little steps are going to get you the lifestyle you want. When you're visualizing things in that state of belief, you actually convince your brain that it's already happening. Your brain cannot tell the difference between reality and visualization. If you do it right, your brain will actually believe that you are already doing all the things. This causes them to happen faster, because your brain uses its powers to create these things, to bring these opportunities to you, so that you can seize them and leverage them in your life.

If you want to be successful, you must believe in your ability to create the things that you desire in life. The life you want is waiting for you to step up and take it. Believe that you can do it, focus on what you really want, desire it with every cell in your body, and then take the actions to create the thing you so desperately want and move Heaven and Earth to get it!

Ask For What You Want

Riches, wealth, ambition, abundance, dreams, goals, accohmplish-ments, success, and achievement all start in the same place—in the mind with a deep desire to have those things. You see, all things that we get or want are created in the mind first, and it is the spark of desire to have them that pushes us to get them.

Desire is the first step in having what you want in this life. You won't work, push, fight, or even die for something without a deep desire to have it. I have seen this in my life many times.

A number of years ago I had a truly deep desire to have something. My wife and I had just had our fourth and fifth children: twins. I was at a job that I enjoyed, but felt I was not making the amount of money I needed to support my family. I was making about $65,000 per year at the time, and we did okay, but I desired to have greater abundance in my life. At the time, I felt that if I could increase my income to $85,000 per year, we would be much better off, and my family would be able to have a more comfortable life.

My wife and I had just learned about vision boards, so one of the first goals I put on my vision board was to get a job making $85,000 per year. The exact wording was, "I have a job making $85,000 per year." Notice the "have" in the wording. I already imagined myself having it. I also had a picture of money raining down. I would look at that picture and read the words every morning and evening before I went to bed. I had a burning desire to find that job and make that money.

A few weeks went by, and as I looked at my vision and my desire, opportunities started to present themselves. A recruiter reached out to me about a job he felt I was qualified for. A past coworker said the company he was working for was looking for someone like me and my expertise at his work. I applied for both jobs, and I got interviews at both.

The first job from the recruiter I was working with called a few days later after the interview. He said I really impressed the people who interviewed me, and they made me an offer. The problem was that the amount of money they wanted to pay me was $68,000, only a few thousand dollars above what I was making, and not close to the $85,000 I wanted. I hadn't heard back from the other company, so I felt they were not interested in making me an offer. I told the recruiter that if I was going to leave where I was, I would need $85,000. He was not happy and told me he did not think that I would be able to get that, but that he would see what he could do. He called me back the next day and said the highest they would go was $80,000, and that was a major stretch for them. I thought about that and felt that maybe with a bonus and overtime and possibly a raise, I would reach that $85,000 in the next year, so I accepted.

I put in my two weeks at my current job, had a start date for my new job, and the very last day of my old job, the other company I had interviewed with called with an offer. They asked me what I was making, and I told them $80,000, because that is what I was going to be making at my new job. They asked if I would be willing to work for them if they paid me $90,000. I was ecstatic. Not only did I reach and surpass my desired income, but the new job was only five minutes from my house, as opposed to thirty minutes for the other job. I accepted the second offer and had to let the other job know I would not be starting on Monday.

I tell you this story to let you know that if you have a true desire and want something badly enough, you can make it happen. It may not always happen the way you think, but it can come to fruition. So have that desire and go after your dreams.

LACEY & ADAM PLATT

About Lacey Platt: Lacey is an energetic, fun loving, super mom of five! She is an Achievement Coach, Speaker and new Bestselling Author who enjoys helping everyone she can by getting to know what their needs are and then loving on them in every way that she can. Her ripple effect and impact has touched the lives of so many and continues to reach more lives every single day. Allow Lacey to help you achieve your goals with proven techniques she has created and perfected over years of coaching. Her and her husband have built an amazing coaching business called Arise to Connect serving people all around the world.

About Adam Platt: Adam is an Achievement Coach, Speaker, Trainer, Podcast Host and now a Bestselling Author. Adam loves to help people overcome the things stopping them from having the life they really want. Adam owns and operates Arise to Connect. Adam believes that connection with yourself, others, and your higher power are the keys to achievement and greater success in life. He is impacting thousands of people's lives with his message and coaching. He lives in Utah with his five daughters and dog, Max.

Author's website: *www.AriseToConnect.com*
Book Series Website & Author's Bio: *www.The13StepsToRiches.com*

Louisa Jovanovich

FOLLOW YOUR DESIRE

Desire means a calling from my heart. Something I feel in my soul. A yearning that just keeps coming up. It is God speaking to me in an experience that feels like what I would call desire. Desire means you get to live a life that inspires others, so they are moved and inspired by who they are and what they want. They get to experience it in their own being because of experiencing it in my energy.

Desire means to make a difference, to experience freedom, joy, love, connection, and an insatiable yearning. My desire is to make a difference in this world, so when someone experiences me, they, too, feel inspired and excited.

I remember being a young girl and not feeling great about being home, so I went off to work. By the time my day was over, I felt excited, alive, and connected. I knew that I desired love and connection and the ability to give and receive it.

In high school, I wanted to go to beauty school. I knew my school offered a program, and I could receive credits to get my cosmetology license, yet my parents said, "No." They wanted me to do something smart with my life. My desire was to become a hairdresser. It came naturally to me, and I felt in my flow the most when I was behind the chair doing hair. I got to connect with clients and give them an experience. Since my parents said no, I used my babysitting money for beauty school and got my license. At twelve years old, I began babysitting and over time saved $11,000. Exactly what it cost to put myself through the program.

I also desired living on my own before marrying. I wanted independence, but being Armenian, I knew that was not in the cards for me. I was to live at home and then marry. It was not what I wanted for my life. I desired being financially free and independent. I desired to work hard, buy a house, and get married. So I worked hard at doing what I love, saving money, and also trying to be the perfect woman for a man, thinking that is exactly how my life would be perfect.

I set out to accomplish that. I followed what I thought I desired, the life I was raised to believe was the right choice. My desire to be a wife and a mother was so strong I did what I could to accomplish that. I did, however, ignore the signs of it not feeling right. My desire to have my life be what I dreamed of was more powerful than the intuition that was trying to come through on who I was choosing as my husband.

At seventeen, I traveled to Florida to visit a friend. I thought I wanted to move there. Later on, my life led me to visit Florida again when my husband's job gave us an opportunity to live there. I reconnected with the desire from my past when we were actually moving to Florida. It was surreal. I really thought it was meant to be, and I do believe everything happens for a reason. It was a desire in my heart to live in Florida, and I love that I was able to manifest it.

I had an incredible time over four years and remember people saying, "Wherever you go, you seem to be very happy." I say, "Wherever you go, you bring yourself along." So while there I was happy. I discovered hot yoga, rode bikes, and participated in a book club. They were amazing experiences I realized I loved. I ended up getting divorced, as my desire for love and freedom was more powerful than my need to stay in a marriage that was not working. My love of feeling free and alive and my desire to be who I truly am will always win.

Then, my heart's desire was to move back to L.A. To be with my parents, my sister, and back with my friends. I didn't know how I was going to make that happen and just sat with the possibility that it was going to happen. I held it in my heart that if it was meant to be, I would be back in L.A. I believed when the time was right, I would do whatever it took to move back.

In the last year, it became possible. COVID became our reality, and I could no longer travel from L.A. to Florida to keep my hairdressing business alive. So, I packed up with my children and headed to L.A. It seemed easy for me, yet people said it was an incredible accomplishment. I love being someone who has always followed my desires. Someone who feels an experience and sees what's possible and makes it come alive. I love being someone others say is inspiring. I enjoy the feedback that my love of following my dreams, known as desire (to me), has people believing they, too, can accomplish their desires.

I experience joy and fulfillment when what I desire is accomplished and the world as I know it feels satisfying. The words" I love" come to mind when I say "desire." Like "I love to…(fill in the blank)." When I do what I love, it feels like I'm connecting with my desires. I live in a state of flow, where intention, love, and desire is where I make my choices from. They are all in alignment with my authenticity. So living and choosing from desire will be a state of connection, love, inspiration, and joy. A world that feels powerful.

Having children was an important desire for me. I was committed to being a mother. I didn't know why; I just knew it was something I needed to do. I knew I wanted so badly to wake up and go to sleep having created a loving family. I knew I had so much love to give, and it was important to share that. However, being a mother was not at all what I thought it would be. I had read the words from famous authors that said *your children come through you, they don't belong to you.* We get to guide them and love them, but they are here on their own mission. They have their own purpose to live and their own desires to fulfill. We just get to look in our mirror and follow our own authentic calling.

A friend said to me she would have paid a million dollars to fix her child. Oh, that sounds so dramatic. *Not* really, if you're honest with yourself. What does it feel like as a parent when we think we know what our child *needs*? We think we are here to create the person who just couldn't get it perfect. To be the ones who don't have shortcomings. Yet they talk back and have the nerve to say "no" to us. God has put special desires in every one of us. We are all here on a mission. That quiet voice that talks to us. How come some hear it more clearly than others? How does your voice show up for you? My voice shows up in a way that makes me physically uncomfortable. I just can't continue with what I'm doing when it's trying to speak to me. It feels like a powerful yearning that will not go away until I listen to it.

Another desire is to experience freedom. So, going back to when I was seventeen, I wanted to meet a friend at the gym at 4 a.m., so I took a shower and got ready. I started heading out of the house around 5 a.m. to get in the car and go, but my dad asked where I was going, and when I said, "To the gym," he said, "NO WAY." I was not allowed to go at that time in the morning. I didn't want to take no for an answer, so I was determined that I was actually going to go. I lost the fight that night because the car belonged to him. My desire for freedom showed up that day. I didn't want to feel controlled, and I needed to feel free. I've done everything in my power to set things up so as not to feel stuck or controlled.

My dad never told me this before, but when we were talking one day, he said he is so grateful that I have always been independent. All of the things in life I have ever set out to do, I was able to accomplish. He has no idea that came from the day he would not let me take his car. When I came to him and said I was going to get a divorce, he said "Okay." He was confident that I was strong and capable. He knew I would be okay on my own. I am so grateful he shared this with me.

LOUISA JOVANOVICH

About Louisa Jovanovich: Louisa is a Transformation Life Coach. She has graduated from Landmark Forum, HCL, Gratitude Training. Louisa is a certified Clarity Catalyst Coach. Louisa has hosted a global summit. Through her individual and group coaching practice, Connect with Source, Louisa intuitively guides adults and teens to gain the clarity they desire to take their lives to the next level. Her clients are consistently successful at shifting their lives and experiencing more joy, abundance, passion, and compassion, by learning how to turn negative beliefs into accountability and self-love. Over her 20-year career, Louisa has helped many people change their perspectives on what is possible for their lives.

Author's website: *www.ConnectWithSource.com*
Book Series Website & Author's Bio: *www.The13StepsToRiches.com*

Maris Segal & Ken Ashby

THE DRIVE UNDERNEATH DESIRE

As infants, we came into this world from desire! Through our youth into our teens and adulthood, everything we have done and continue to do in our personal and professional lives stems from desire. From the time our alarm goes off in the morning until our heads hit the pillow to sleep, and from cradle to grave, "desire" is a human driver. Our desire to succeed, connect, love, and lead is very personal and sparks our emotions. When our individual desires match up with others, the powerful becomes possible.

When we approached writing this chapter on "desire," our initial thoughts immediately gravitated to our 24/7 desires around our life as husband and wife and our business partnership, which connects us in an omnipresent way. Now, you may be thinking initially that we mean physical desire, as that's what often comes up for many when hearing the word "desire": a romantic relationship, but it goes much deeper!

We see desire as a holistic 360-degree approach to our entire lives, personal and professional. The desire we feel for each other comes from the depths of our being. The desire to collaborate, the desire to learn from each other, the desire to explore and be continuously curious, the desire to lead and serve to make the world a better place, and the desire to play together and lead our family with love all come from this depth. This embodiment of desire is natural, passionate, collaborative, raw, emotional, and complete. All of the above came rushing into our heads, hearts, and bodies in a New York minute when we heard the word "desire." What comes to you when you think of "desire" in your own life?

Every human on the planet arrives to the present from a place of desire. In fact, your desire to read this book brings us here to this moment today. As part of our business strategy and leadership work, we coach our clients that success at any age, whether it be at home or at work, can be realized when desire is combined with "DRIVE"—Declaration, Relationships, Intention, Vision, Excellence. Desire, alone, is not enough!

Here's how it works: when we recognize our desire, we *Declare* our desire to ourselves and enroll those we have *Relationships* with colleagues, family, friends who may support bringing our desire to fruition. We then set our *Intention* and *Vision* then build and follow a plan and complete in *Excellence*. "DRIVE." We know from history that one person's desire can build up and tear down nations, companies, families, and communities. One person's desire can create world-class athletes and humanitarians, as well as tyrants. One person's desire can spark collaborations and build a movement. Desire soars with wings of possibilities!

KEN: I am the son of a Southern Baptist preacher and grew up in rural Kentucky. Being preacher's kids, my younger sister and I were living into my father's desire to be a minister and we were in a church pew whenever the doors were open. My father and mother instilled in us the desire to be close to family and be in service to others—powerful life lessons which have continued to guide me throughout my journey of life.

As a teenager, I worked as a field hand for the tobacco harvest, played basketball, and was in nine different schools before I graduated. With each new environment, I felt a desire to connect and belong. I am certain my parents wanted me to "answer the call" like my dad, but that was their desire, not mine.

I recall that my first real desire came in the form of music. I was invited to participate in a local talent contest, and I had the *drive* to compete as a singer, and that sparked the fire of desire to be a musician. While I was attending college, an unexpected opportunity landed on my doorstep. It was as though the Universe was enrolled in my desire. I left home, school, and family to travel as a student with the global youth leadership organization, Up with People. The opportunity to perform music all over the world that was inclusive of all cultures and ethnicities perfectly matched my vision of using my musical and vocal talents for the greater good.

I took a leap of faith, jumped headfirst, and little did I know that this was the first major step in fulfilling my desire, and it changed my life in so many magnificent ways. As our cast traveled, music became my expression, and I began writing songs about almost everything I encountered: a host family, a fellow cast member, or a town in which we were performing. This desire resulted in hundreds of original song collaborations, which were, in time, performed live around the world for millions of people from heads of households to Heads of State. That fire of desire from my youth continues to carry into our work today.

MARIS: I am the youngest of three girls and grew up in New Jersey and Florida. My youth was spent in a fairly traditional Jewish upbringing. My paternal grandmother lived nearby, so our holidays were joyfully spent at her home at the Jersey Shore with aunts, uncles, and cousins. My parents' desire to instill the beauty, roots, and traditions of our faith led my sisters and me to a truly rich experience during our thirteen years in private Hebrew school. Sharing our culture and learning from others was a constant desire that kept me curious and exploring.

My parents' professional lives afforded us great opportunities to meet people from all walks of life. My dad, an avid athlete, had been a fighter pilot early in their marriage, and then he lived his life as an entrepreneur whose desires took him across the globe and back home to share stories with our family. My mom's desire to heal people began with her job as a parole officer. Then, after earning her master's in clinical social work, her career as a therapist and mental health activist took flight.

Immersed from my youth in civic engagement, arts, and sports, my desires have always centered around connecting, healing, and uniting diverse populations.

How did Ken and I find our way to each other from such diverse backgrounds? The answer is: desire and timing! *Together, we believe that we are where we are when we are meant to be.* Like Ken, I also saw Up with People as a teen and met members of the cast who were being hosted by family friends. After seeing over one hundred students from twenty plus countries on stage motivating an audience of strangers to link arms and connect with the music, I knew where my desire and future would take me next. I traveled as a student in a cast and then worked for the organization across the United States, Mexico, and abroad. As I was being hosted by generous families in hundreds of communities large and small from three room homes with dirt floors to mansions, I was constantly struck by the shared desires of strangers who, like us as students, were hungry to explore cultures, share perspectives, and create meaningful connections. In each community these shared desires created lasting friendships, and after just a few days, we were no longer strangers. Ken and I only met briefly during this time, and many years later, we reconnected. This experience of collaborating with shared desires remains the foundation of my life and our life together.

Our shared desire to impact lives has taken us from classrooms to boardrooms, from the Olympics to Super Bowl halftime shows, and from Popes to Presidents. In each case, we have served as the "connection couple," known for matching desires with purpose and creating memorable "now" moments for people around the world. Fast forward to the world of COVID-19, as a couple, we have renewed our recognition that life is fragile, life is now, and desire and DRIVE invites us to step into our vision to be a couple engaged in connected coaching.

The balance and prioritization of our desires in our personal and professional lives is paramount. This is not a JOB; this is the work we love. Our DRIVE to follow our desires that make an impact has supported us in bringing a creative voice to brands, issues, and causes, and to unite diverse populations across the globe. Now, having experienced the pandemic pause, we have refocused our desire to support, in our being, the possibility of global consciousness and the recognition that we all, as human beings, are connected. Together, we are committed to continue to fan this fire of desire in everyone we encounter and to embrace life's joyful and turbulent moments together, always holding on to our shared humanity.

Our world has seen times when injustices have prevailed, when a pandemic has taken precious lives, when social impact and service has illuminated both a greater connection and a myth of division. As we continue our work, we can see in the eyes of our niece, nephews, and grandchildren, a new generation that will lead us into a brighter tomorrow, based on their *desires* and supported by the *drive* underneath, declarations, relationships, intention, vision, and excellence.

In the end, fulfilling our desires is not a decision, it's a choice!

Reflections:

1. Describe your current desires and how they align with your life?

2. How does fulfilling your desire look and feel to you?

3. In what ways is your DRIVE supporting your desire?

MARIS SEGAL & KEN ASHBY

About Marls Segal and Ken Ashby: Maris Segal and Ken Ashby have been bringing a creative collaborative voice to issues, causes and brands for over forty years. As strategists, producers, coaches, authors, speakers and trainers, their work with the public and private sectors unites diverse populations across a wide spectrum of business, policy, and social issues in the U.S. and abroad. Their leadership expertise in Business Relationship Marketing, Organizational Change & Cultural Inclusion, Personal Growth, Project Management, Public Affairs, Corporate Social Responsibility and Philanthropy Strategies has been called on to support a range of clients from classrooms and boardrooms to the world stage including; Olympic organizers, Super Bowls, Harvard Kennedy School, Papal visits, the White House, consumer brands, and celebrities across the arts and entertainment, sports and culinary genres.

Ken Ashby and Maris Segal recently launched Segal Leadership Global—a community of collaborative strategists, coaches and trainers creating global connections and possibilities in times of change and One Song—a creative music and song writing leadership workshop series designed as a collaboration team building tool.

Often referred by their clients as the "Connection Couple," their philosophy is "our shared humanity unites us and when we lead with our hearts, our heads will follow.

Author's website: *www.SegalLeadershipGlobal.com*
Book Series Website & Author's Bio: *www.The13StepsToRiches.com*

Mel Mason

WALK THROUGH PAIN TO DISCOVER YOUR PURPOSE

Have you ever purchased a new, uncluttered electronic device, only to find the memory full and the performance lagging a year later? Ever cleaned up a room, only to find the surfaces brimming with knick-knacks in no time? Or maybe you've patched up a relationship, only to find things plunging back into the red zone as soon as you turn your back. Clutter builds up in all areas of life, despite our best intentions. But most people don't consider the dangerous effect this can have on our deepest desires.

As we go through life, we want things. We set goals, but then, we see more stuff we want. We get confused, with desires pulling us in all directions. As a child, we can't decide whether we want to be a star in soccer or math class. Is trapeze more important to us, or cello? When we get older, this problem only intensifies. We really care about getting promoted, running an ultramarathon, and being an awesome parent, all while investing in the next Facebook, building our own sailboat, dominating the local party scene, and perfecting our golf game. As our desires become cluttered, we lose effectiveness. We won't get anything we want if we can't decide what we value most.

Often, we choose confusing and harmful desires to distract ourselves from the emotional baggage from something difficult that happened. We don't want to face the dark thoughts, nor even acknowledge them. So, we busy ourselves chasing meaningless things, instead. *Just stay busy, and we won't have to think about it.*

You may desire wealth and spend your days chasing riches to distract yourself from trauma. Or maybe you keep yourself busy caring for others, so you don't have to face a void within. You are loved (and rich, too). But the trauma never disappears. It's making you sick with self-hate, because you never decided what to do with it. The trauma is a hideous bookmark cemented into one page of your life, and you can't turn the page, because you refuse to look down at the book.

I know a thing or two about avoiding trauma. When I was child, I was sexually and emotionally abused. Then my parents divorced, and my world was split in two. The trauma was too much for my little body to handle… and then, my brother committed suicide.

When I lost my brother, the one person who'd been with me through everything, I broke. I went through the dark night of my soul. I became obsessed with death. I was ready to leave this planet at any moment, and I didn't believe I mattered. I thought I was broken beyond repair.

So, I did what any sensible person would do: I tried not to think about it.

When you avoid trauma; however, it ends up on a torturous loop in your head. It replays itself endlessly in the background of your mind, whether you like it or not. I didn't know it at the time, but I was playing the loop of my brother's suicide and the unspeakable memories of my abuse like a broken record. I was frightened of connecting with others and the world that spit me out. One day, I heard the sound of truth.

Truth is the most beautiful sound in the world. When you hear the truth, every sense in your body becomes alive. The first truth I ever believed whole-heartedly was that we are all brothers and sisters, because we came from the same father. When I was five, and my parents had just split, I was thinking about how sad I was. Then, all of a sudden, my body became light, and I had a moment of clarity. I realized God was the connection of all people. My parents no longer lived in the same home, but we would still all be connected. I didn't lose anyone. We were all one.

Many of the truths we learn as adults were once clear to us as children. We are born connected to God. Then, we go through some knocks in life, and we forget.

When I was a teenager, I went to a little souvenir shop in Salisbury Beach that sold shell figurines, keychains, and magnets. I was browsing around, my trauma playing on repeat, thinking about ending it all soon. And then, I saw this little shell frame with the "Footprints" poem placed in it—I know you've seen it—that famous allegorical poem about God abandoning you in tough times with the image of one set of footprints. It's about that question we ask God because we're so mad at our impossible fate, "Why did you leave me during this trauma? I needed you!"

And the Lord has this to say: "My precious child, I would never leave you. During times of trial and suffering, when you see only one set of footprints, that's when I carried you."

Standing there in that souvenir shop, I again heard that old truth I'd stuffed away in my subconscious. It was the same, clear belief I had when I was five. I remembered I was part of the human family, and all of us came from one source.

I wasn't going through this for nothing. My trauma would be used for a higher purpose. I suddenly knew my core desire in life was to remind others we are all connected. From that day on, I knew I needed to walk through my pain. I was going to declutter my desires. I wanted to get past the superficial. It was time to suit up and *show up*. My thoughts of suicide faded, because my deep desire to share my suffering was more powerful.

It's been a winding journey, but the poem kept me alive. It helped me realize we are all connected in suffering. I wasn't alone.

Every day is a risk. It's easy to crawl back into your clutter. Staying connected to your deepest desires is a constant practice. What helps you recognize we are all connected in suffering, like I did with the "Footprints" poem?

Today, I've developed an arsenal of activities that keep me grounded in the present (like meditating and hiking) and help me connect with others (like Reiki energy healing). That's what makes me feel like a positive participant on Team Earth. For you, it might be fishing in a lake or sitting under the stars. How do you declutter and reconnect with what matters most?

It's not hard. It could be meditation, prayer, or just sitting still for one freaking second—whatever brings you inward. Get past the superficial and clear the clutter from your head. What lines up with this moment? The answer is sitting right there on your chest. Breathe it. What has your suffering led you to desire out of this life?

You don't need a medium to channel your higher self to find your life's purpose. It's right there! Ask yourself what you really desire. You are on your way to manifesting that very thing that makes you feel connected.

The power of nature always gets me back on track. I don't have to go far to find it. Even in the city, you can find a quiet place under the shade of a planted tree in the middle of a sidewalk, or on the grass in the park. If you're experiencing trauma right now, go to a memory or image that makes you feel good. To endure concentration camps, Holocaust survivors imagined the natural beauty of their hometown landscapes, and the ripe flavors of the foods they loved. Find a quiet place to imagine what you desire most.

Right outside my door is a gorgeous mountain speckled with palm trees. Each day, I grab some fresh air, go hiking, walk the neighborhood, or sit in my backyard. I love to ask myself the big questions: What is keeping me alive? Is what I'm chasing right now in sync with my values? How has my suffering fueled my core desire?

How you can recognize your desire:
- Remember this truth: We are all one. And just like that R.E.M. song: *Everybody Hurts.*

- Go to a place that makes you feel connected.
- Walk through your pain and find the meaning in it.
- Declutter the superficial desires you are chasing.
- Commit to your core desire, and let it be your guiding force.
- Practice connection in the way that speaks to you.
- Decide to live.

MEL MASON

About Mel Mason: International Best-Selling Author Mel Mason is The Clutter Expert, and as a sexual abuse survivor, she grew up depressed, suicidal, and surrounded by clutter. What she realized after coming back from the brink of despair and getting through her own chaos was that the outside is just a mirror of the inside, and if you only address the outside without changing the inside, the clutter keeps coming back.

That set her on a mission to empower people around the world to get free from clutter inside and out, so they can experience happiness and abundance in every area of their lives.

She is the author of *Freedom from Clutter: The Guaranteed, Foolproof, Step-by-Step Process to Remove the Stuff That's Weighing You Down*

Author's website: *www.FreeGiftFromMel.com*
Book Series Website & Author's Bio: *www.The13StepsToRiches.com*

Dr. Miatta Hampton

THE FEELING OF DESIRE

The feeling to want more, to do something different, to become something greater was a sort of yearning that I could not explain. To walk in the potential and power that I was created for can be defined as desire. My desire was the thing that guided my intentions and goals and fueled my actions. My desire placed a demand on me to level up in life.

When I realized I was in a remedial English class in high school, I was embarrassed and confused. The weight of knowing I was not in a regular English class was more than my fourteen-year-old mind could handle. It was through no one's fault but my own. I had not applied myself. My experiences in my education left me feeling inadequate and insignificant. I did not think I was smart enough, so why try? Instead of reading through the questions on my high school entrance exam, I doodled on the scantron sheet and made patterns, like the letter "C."

Now, I regretted it. I wanted out of this class, I wanted more. I thought to myself, *I can do more. I can be more.* My own negative thoughts about myself landed me in a place I did not want to be in. I allowed what people thought about me to become the deciding factor of who I would be. I was fully capable of more. I decided to challenge myself and to create a plan to get out of that class.

I had settled for what people thought I was capable of. If I stayed in this place, my self-confidence would continue to shrink. I decided to stop accepting less than what I deserved. I had a goal, and what I was being offered was not good enough for what I desired or for where I was headed. I had been in this box far too long.

I learned that people love putting you in a box. It is the thing that makes them feel comfortable. If you want change, you must create it. No one was offering any solutions or a way out of this situation. Everyone seemed comfortable with the way things were going except me. My hopes, my dreams, and my future depended on me changing the course of my educational experience.

Attending nursing school was a new experience for me. My desire for success and a better life brought me to this current door, and I decided to walk through it with confidence and boldness. I earned a right to be here. Nothing would stand in my way of completing my Bachelor of Science in Nursing (BSN) degree and becoming a registered nurse (RN). I had got it in my mind that I wanted that degree. I wanted those letters, "RN."

I was willing to sacrifice time, money, energy, sleep, and comfort. If I was going to achieve my dreams, I could not waste time hanging out with friends and spending extra money. I had to invest my time studying and my money paying for tuition. There was going to be a cost. Either way I looked at it, there would be a cost. Every time I thought about quitting, I asked myself, *How much would it cost you to not pursue your purpose?*

My first year in nursing school was a challenge. I was uncomfortable with my level of understanding of the information. I felt like everyone was getting it except me. My professor did not make it any easier, making snide remarks about my ability to successfully complete the program. My desire had given me a seat in the nursing program. I was determined that I would not allow my fear of failing to get in the way of this opportunity. I had mentally prepared myself for the road ahead. I planned for the nights that I would have to stay up drinking coffee and studying, writing papers, and eating noodles for dinner. I could see myself walking across the stage while they called my name to receive my BSN.

That wasn't enough. Here I sat on the phone annoyed, devastated, discouraged, and disappointed. I had been kicked out of nursing school. Not because I did not show up, not because I did not do the work, but because I failed to apply the knowledge. As the saying goes "knowledge is power"—well, that is not entirely true. I had the knowledge; the problem was I did not know how to apply it. I had all the information, I just did not know what to do with it, how to make it convert, and I felt penalized. I thought it was a stupid rule and could not believe what I was hearing. I tried to think of all the ways I could appeal the decision.

In order to pass for the semester, I needed a 76% average on class work and the final exam. I had an 80% for class work but a 75.9% on the final exam. I was being kicked out for a tenth of a point. I was told I had to reapply. Imagine being that close and being told, "Sorry, we do not round up." I had invested time, money, and energy. I had gone days with minimal sleep. School had cost me relationships, and for what? To fail?

I thought back to high school when I felt stuck and trapped in that high school remedial English class. I thought, *Who am I kidding? I will never be smart enough.* All those negative thoughts came rushing back to my mind. I was not going to be content with the outcome. I had a goal and the thought of failing was not an option. No more settling for what people thought I was capable of. I am fully capable of more.

Failing intensified my desire. I was not going to be denied the opportunity to change my life. I reapplied and submitted an action plan that detailed how I would matriculate through the program and exactly how long it would take me to do it. That day, I learned to never underestimate the power of a determined mind. When you are told "no," turn that "no" into a new opportunity. I had the ability to navigate an uncomfortable situation.

Reflecting on a conversation I had with my ninth grade English teacher, she encouraged me to never settle for what people think I can do.

I asked her, "Do I have to be in a remedial class next year?"

Her response would have an impact on my life for years to come. She replied, "Absolutely not, and I believe you have what it takes to successfully transition."

In that moment, I realized I could do whatever I put my mind to. Those simple words sparked belief in myself, and I continue to draw on them daily.

Surprise yourself and dream big. The best way to overcome setbacks is to regulate them, adapt to them, and bring them into submission with your positive thoughts about who you are and what you are capable of. It is vital that you maintain a positive attitude. For every negative thing you say to yourself, say two positive things.

What do you really want? To start a business? To write a book? Finish college? Leave your nine-to-five? Write it down, and be specific; do not leave your life to chance. Place your wants on a sheet of paper, and post them in an area of your house that you pass daily. Every morning, go to that place and read your wants out loud to yourself. If you want to take it a step further, write down how you plan to make those things happen.

I want to generate $50,000 a month in passive income by December 2025. I want to take my family on vacation whenever, create memories, and not have to ask permission to do it. I will create action steps annually, quarterly, and monthly to stay on task to see my desires turn to reality. My secret weapon to achieving my desires are to prioritize, set goals, have self-discipline, have an open mind and to not lean on my own understanding but in all my ways acknowledge God and He will direct my path (Proverbs 3:5). Although at times, things may not work out the way I intend for them, I will remain positive, have patience, operate with wisdom, have faith, and will not doubt.

Believe in yourself, your dreams, and your ability. Desire is necessary to achieve your dreams. It will lead you to your purpose. You can do whatever you desire with faith and persistence. Go to work with what you have, stop waiting for the right time, the right moment, or the right people. Affirm yourself, and start now!!!

DR. MIATTA HAMPTON

About Dr. Miatta Hampton: Dr. Miatta Hampton is a nurse leader, #1 Best-Selling Author, speaker, coach, and minister. Miatta impacts others with her powerful, relatable messages of pursing purpose, and she empowers her audiences to live life on purpose and according to their dreams. She coaches and inspires women to turn chaos into cozy, pivot to prosperity, and how to profit in adversity. Miatta provides tools and resources for personal, professional, and financial growth.

Author's website: *www.DrMiattaSpeaks.com*
Book Series Website & Author's Bio: *www.The13StepsToRiches.com*

Michael D. Butler

FINDING YOUR FOUNTAIN OF YOUTH

The idea of the Fountain of Youth has its origins in creation, when mankind was exiled from the Garden of Eden, and runs deep in the hearts of humans everywhere throughout the generations forward and backwards for thousands of years.

The Spanish Explorer, Ponce de León tried to find it, and plastic surgeons sell it *en masse* in a bottle, capsule, retreat, or surgery. Most everyone wants to look and feel great, so it's a huge market and always will be.

Born with Desire

The desire to live, grow, and prosper are placed within all of us before birth. The desire to walk, build, grow, and learn that grows into the desire to connect, love, create children, and leave a legacy never stops developing until we die. The desire to travel, explore, and discover new things currently has the human race pursuing the colonization of Mars and the Moon. Humans desire change over time, but the constant desire is the need for growth and expansion. The DNA of success is the divine thumbprint of an Almighty Creator, and as humans, each of us possess it.

At age eighteen, I was ready to leave the house and start my life. Putting my name on the lease in college meant I could be the landlord and collect rent from my two college roommates. It also meant I was responsible for the rent if they did not pay. I desired freedom and discovered it was found in responsibility. Many in modern psychology will argue that desire cannot be changed; I disagree. I look at my own life and see how I fine-tuned and even changed my desires by changing my vision.

Desire Can Be Good or Bad

Desire is not evil or good. It is a God-given characteristic we are all born with. Some choose to use desire for evil, while others choose to use it for good. Desire—like hunger, the need for sleep, the drive for sex, and the drive to succeed—is neither good nor evil. Desire is normal and natural. The ethics and motives of desire can be judged in how humans choose to use their desire. For example, a parent can desire one path for their child, but true bliss will come for the parent and the child once the parent recognizes the uniqueness in their child and allows the child to make choices for themselves as they age - Experiencing the positive and the negative results of their choices.

How to Change Your Desire

How do we change someone's desire? We change their picture. Growing up in communist Poland, eight-year-old Ania's family had to wait in line weekly for toilet paper, flour, and salt. Fast forward a decade-and-a-half later, living on the beach in Naples, Florida, she would see how another side of life could be—the life of the affluent and the wealthy. She would quickly attain her goals by putting herself through college and going on to get her Master's and Doctoral degrees, opening a wellness spa, and opening a women's high-end fashion boutique that would bring former presidents of the U.S., other nations, and the famed fashion designer Oscar de la Renta into her store.

The Wright Brothers

Kittyhawk, North Carolina is the place the Wright brothers took their idea—flying a plane, and tested it to find eleven seconds of success. They did, indeed, go airborne, but only for eleven seconds. Many would call that a failure. They, however, saw it as a resounding success. Their vision for flight fuels our world economy to this day. I step on dozens of airplanes around the globe in a single month. The Wright Brothers defied the law of gravity with a greater law: the law of lift.

Desire Begins with Vision

My desire to run my first marathon was reborn in me at age thirty-nine-and-a-half. I had written it down as a bucket list goal when I was thirty and almost forgot about it. But when I ran across that notebook of bucket list items, the desire in me was reborn. I could feel, hear, and see myself crossing the finish line with my arms in the air and the crowd cheering.

Running My First Marathon

That very day, I laced up my shoes and ran one block and was out of breath. The next morning, I ran a block and two mailboxes, and I was gasping for air. I immediately knew what I needed to do.

That very second, I went home and googled "new running shoes," but I didn't stop there. I found and joined a running group in my city where three times a week and every Saturday morning at five or six a.m., we'd meet and do our long runs.

Laser Focus Mixed with Burning Desire

Running coaches will tell you that the optimal journey from "couch potato" to marathoner should take at least a year, depending on your age. I only gave myself six months to train, because my fortieth birthday was approaching, and it was my desire on my bucket list to complete my marathon before the age of forty.

Working with a Team of Mentors

I considered my running group of twenty young athletes—yes, I was the oldest in my group—to be my team of mentors. Most of them had run at least one marathon, and our coach had run more than 100. Even though I spent most of my time trying to catch up with "the pack," they pulled me—kicking and screaming at times—to new heights in my health, which would translate into business and in life.

There's no way I could have endured the long training runs of eighteen and twenty miles without them. The pain, the passion, and the fun conversations propelled me and motivated me to get out of bed at five a.m. on Saturday mornings in the twenty degree weather, because I knew they would hold me accountable. More importantly, I was holding myself accountable. The idea of the sheer boredom or running without them and the feeling of loneliness one experiences running alone fueled me to press myself to run 26.2 miles. I never could have done it without them.

Not only did I finish my first marathon, The Route 66 Marathon in Tulsa, Oklahoma before my fortieth birthday, but my four sons—Michael, Matthew, Joshua, and Jeremiah—all ran the last three miles with me, crossing the finish line with me, making that—apart from the days my sons were born—my greatest life moment ever.

What Do You Desire?

What is it you desire? What is it you want in life? What is it you really want? Go ahead and think about it for a moment. Close your eyes and visualize it. Ask yourself, *What do I really want?* Now, begin to see yourself achieving it. Write it down, speak about it, talk about it. Visualize it. Dream about it. Write it down and post it to your mirror and your refrigerator and inside your car and on your phone as your screen saver. Jim Rohn said, "We become what we think about most of the time." King Solomon said in Proverbs, "As a man/woman thinks in their heart, so are they.

I love the story of Caleb, the eighty-year-old patriarch in the Bible who told Moses, "Give me this mountain" that was promised to him at age forty. Many would have given up if they had not realized their dream in forty years, but not Caleb. Regardless of his age, he was still ready and willing to receive all that had been promised to him and his children. No matter what your age or station in life, now is the time to start, and don't give up until you have it!

Visualize what you want and take the necessary steps to achieve your dream, regardless of your setbacks or failure. Keep looking at the picture you have created, and keep moving forward.

In 1950, no one had ever run a four-minute mile. In fact, experts globally conceded that it would never happen, and the human body was not capable of running a mile in less than four minutes. But in the 1952 Olympics, in Helsinki, Finland, a twenty-three-year-old Brit named Bannister ran a 3:59.4 mile and forever changed the world's mindset about that topic.

He would only hold this coveted title for forty-six days, because, over the next year, more than 100 men ran a sub-four-minute mile, all because the glass ceiling of belief was shattered, and they believed they could. Once belief ignites, desire is born!

MICHAEL D. BUTLER

About Michael D. Butler: Michael Butler has been a guest on Fox News and USA Today and has gotten his clients onto CNN, Dr. Phil, TMZ, TLC, Rolling Stone, Entrepreneur Magazine, Inc500, TBN, TruTV, Fox Business and many others.

His Podcast, The Publisher Podcast is heard by thousands globally and features guests from Hollywood and the Literary Industry.

He has published 4 of his own International best-selling books in multiple languages: *The Single Dad's Survival Guide, Best-Seller Status – Becoming a Best-Selling Author in the Digital Age, The Speaker's Edge – Turning Your Part-Time Passion into Your Full-Time Speaking Career and It's Complicated – When Finding Love was a Matter of Letting Go.*

He Founded and runs 1040Impact.org that rescues kids in human trafficking, educates them and teaches them trade skills to equip them for life in Asia in places like Pakistan.

He is the CEO of Beyond Publishing with authors in 20 countries and over 400 titles by end of 2021.

Author's website: *www.MichaelDButler.com*
Book Series Website & Author's Bio: *www.The13StepsToRiches.com*

Michelle Cameron Coulter & Al Coulter

INSPIRING POSSIBILITIES AND PUSHING PAST YOUR LIMITS

Desire is in every one of us. When you know in your core that nothing can stop you, you're going to figure it out.

"The earth is two-thirds water. You're going to come in contact with it one of these days, so you'd better learn how to swim!"
—Jackie Cameron, my Mom

Growing up in a blended family of ten kids, learning how to swim was mandatory. The biggest challenge was that I was so afraid of the water that I failed my first level of swimming *four* times! On my fourth try, we had to jump in the deep end. I turned around to grab for the side of the pool, and *Boom!*—I cracked my chin on the edge and quickly sank to the bottom of the pool. At the bottom, I totally relaxed, it was peaceful, and I floated up to the surface. When we totally relax, we will float. When we are stressed and *fearful,* we sink. What a huge life lesson. Never would anyone have thought that this quiet, shy, sickly little kid who was so afraid would go on to win an Olympic Gold Medal in synchronized *swimming*!

Starting my sport late, at thirteen years old, I had great role models and mentors.

A couple years later, I made the senior B swim team only because they needed another swimmer. I had a deep desire to keep improving, and never swam to try and beat anyone; instead, focusing on doing a little better every day, and the results started to come.

Coaches and judges started to say, "We didn't realize she had that much potential," and neither did I. I started moving up the ranks, and my confidence started to grow. Confidence comes from doing!

In my first big international competition, I was the alternate on the team. The coach committed that the top eight of the ten swimmers would swim in the team finals. To my surprise, I came eighth by .05 seconds of a point. The coach announced she was keeping the original team, as it was too close. Then, I did something I had never done before: I stood up for myself and talked to the coach. The original eight did end up swimming, which I was grateful for, as I was scared she would have said yes, and a part of me did not feel ready. For the first time, my coach saw in me the feisty desire I had to play bigger.

Two years later, I was paired with the top swimmer in our club. We were training eight hours a day. Weeks before our first World Championship, my coach stopped me in the middle of practice and said, "How would you do it if you were *already* a World Champion?" Wow! Pivotal moment.

Our main competition was identical twins that had been swimming together as a pair for sixteen years, and the championships took place in their hometown pool with ten thousand spectators. Against all the odds, we won our first World Championships.

We would go on to be undefeated three years in a row, until a pre-Olympic meet, months before the Olympic games in Seoul, Korea. We went back to the drawing board; we analyzed our strengths, and we focused on what made us better.

With the world watching, I caught one set of eyes in the stands of thousands right before we swam—it was my mom. The Olympic Gold Medal would be ours.

The desire to be the best I could be was a driving force. Now, my desire is to support others to step into their greatness, to tap into their own Gold Medal potential and do so in a *holistic* way.

Because for years, I held a dark secret ...

I had dealt with an eating disorder the last five years of my swimming career.

I continued to struggle with it for ten years after my swimming career, and it was having my kids that changed my life and started my healing.

My fear in my sharing "my secret" was that I would feel unworthy of my accomplishments in sport and beyond. The opposite happened. I am more connected, stronger, empowered, authentic, and real. I'm honored to inspire others to be their best, explore their incredible possibilities, let go of perfection, and *know that they are more than worthy and have everything it takes.*

Inspiring possibilities and the Gold Medal Potential we all have. We can create greatness in our lives, reach beyond what we thought possible, and pursue it in a real, meaningful, and sustainable way. We even get to have FUN on the journey.

Being a champion is not about being the best in the world— It IS about being the best we can be and being Real in the process.

Now, I get to introduce you to my husband, Al Coulter. We met in Venezuela at the Pan-American games and started going out a year later, on and off for seven years before we got married, as we were both traveling different parts of the world with our sports. This is a part of his story:

I grew up with five siblings, and everyone played hockey as children. My dad always flooded the backyard, so we had a rink to play on. My younger brother went on to play in the NHL. I matured late and was one of the smallest members of our hockey team in ninth grade.

During a playoff game, one of the larger players crushed me into the boards, and after a devastating broken leg, doctors recommended a year off sports. Back then, my only reason for going to school was to play sports, so taking a year off was not going to happen.

As soon as I had played any sport, I always had the desire to do better and be the best I could be and learn how to win at that sport. I discovered volleyball in tenth grade, as they were a player short to start a junior team. I enjoyed the game, but then had a serious injury in the fall of the next two years that almost ended my volleyball career.

First, after making the senior team in eleventh grade, I was riding my bike home, excited to tell my parents I made the team. I had a terrible crash and ended up with eighty stitches to my face and in critical condition in the hospital. Again, doctors said I should take time off from sports, but my desire was so strong I ended up playing in the city finals a few weeks later.

By twelfth grade, I was one of the better players in the province, and at the very first high school league game, I landed on a big player's foot at the net and dislocated my foot right off of my leg. I was raced to the hospital and put in a cast, and guess what the doctors told me? Yes, you will have to take some time off of sports and miss the rest of the season. I ended up playing the City Championships with a cast on, and we won. The game became my passion, and it showed. I was on the junior national team that won Canada's first international medal ever. Then I made the national team.

While on the national team, Al became known as the *Ironman* of volleyball, playing on Team Canada for thirteen years, two Olympics, and Captain of Team Canada his last five years. Al holds the world record in any sport for representing one's country for the most international matches by competing in over 735 international matches for Canada.

Al has been a passionate coach for years now on and off the court. One of my favorite stories is of a group of fifteen-year-old boys who were all cut from different teams. He decided that was way too young to say these kids did not have potential. He started a team just for them. By the end of the season, they ended up placing third out of sixty teams. Their unstoppable desire and someone who believed in them was the magic formula.

Al and I have been together almost thirty-eight years, married thirty. We have gone through the rollercoaster ride called life, with our marriage almost ending at our ten-year mark. It was an intentional decision, work, and desire that turned us around. It has been a constant growing journey since then. We are grateful for our four amazing children, now all young adults. Parenthood has taught us more about life than we could ever imagine, and yes, they are all volleyball players, too—all going through post-secondary school playing the sport they love, and our oldest even playing on the national team and pro.

So what is that deep down desire for you? It can be messy, and you may not know how you are going to get there...you just know. That is desire. Burn, baby, burn. That is the fuel that will take you there.

MICHELLE CAMERON COULTER & AL COULTER

About Michelle Cameron Coulter: Michelle is an Olympic gold medalist, entrepreneur, mother of four, community leader raising millions of dollars for charities, global inspirational leader, and founder and CEO of Inspiring Possibilities.

About Al Coulter: Al is a two-time Olympian in volleyball, captain of Team Canada, world record holder in matches representing one's country in any sport, with over 735 matches, entrepreneur, father of four, and personal best coach, specializing in relationships, team, and resilience.

Michelle and Al are the embodiment of today's leaders. Strong and empowering, they embraced life's challenges with strength and courage. They bring insight, compassion, depth, and inspiration to the table with multiple world championships, three Olympics, an Olympic gold medal, marriage, and four children.

They are sought-after inspirational leaders. Through their speaking, workshops, and retreats, their gift and passion is to inspire possibilities and support people to embrace their greatness in a real, authentic, healthy, and vibrant way—creating thriving community, connection, and one's own gold medal results.

Author's website: *www.MichelleCameronCoulter.com*
Book Series Website & Author's Bio: *www.The13StepsToRiches.com*

IS YOUR GRASS GREEN?

You probably have heard the expression: "The grass is always greener on the other side of the fence." I learned early in life that the concept of "the grass is always greener" works regardless of which side of the fence you are on.

I was born in the late 1960s, the fourth child of a career United States Air Force military man. I spent my childhood in my mother's home country of the Philippines, where my father was stationed at Clark Air Base. My elder brothers and sister had lived in America before I was born. They told me stories of the grand cities and how different life was in the U.S.A. I was a young American who had never seen America. Up to this point in my life, I had only experienced a tiny third-world country in the Pacific Ocean. I would look at the map of the world to compare the Philippine Islands to the United States. It baffled me that any land mass could be so vast.

My vision of American life was formed primarily by television, movies, and magazines. My naïve view of American life fueled a large part of my childhood daydreams. Imagine the rose-colored impression I held with views created from television shows like

Leave it to Beaver, The Brady Bunch, The Courtship of Eddie's Father, The Carol Burnett Show, and *The Dick Van Dyke Show.* My expectation of family life was that at the end of the day, every mishap or situation would be settled. The house was always immaculately clean, organized, and dinner magically appeared out of ovens fully garnished and ready to eat.

My glorified impression was amplified to spectacular heights through movies involving Elvis Presley, Gene Kelly, Fred Astaire, Judy Garland, and the Rat Pack. The streets were clean, the buildings were spectacular, and if you were ever to break into song, everyone around you would sing along and dance in unison, like a flash mob. Disney musicals created the additional bonus feature of animated creatures joining into the fun.

Magazines like *Vogue, Woman's Day, Good Housekeeping,* and *Reader's Digest* further created images of beauty, glamour and insightfulness that fascinated my young mind. The women in America were glamorous, tall, and nothing like me. They all looked like Barbie™ dolls. Their flawless faces, big hair, and graceful demeanor were not what I saw in my island world. Women I knew were usually working hard, scrubbing, sweating, moving quickly through their activities, their hair up in makeshift buns with tendrils of stray hairs framing their sweat-glistened faces.

The recipes in the magazines were always for huge pieces of meat with brightly colored side dishes. In the Philippines, we would have a much smaller portion of meat, usually cut into bite-sized pieces, combined into large pots of savory goodness which incorporated vegetables, along with a large side of steamed rice. I must admit, my impressions of American food did not surpass what I saw before me on a daily basis.

The stories, mysteries, and jokes in *Reader's Digest* fueled the illusion that people in America were exciting, sleuth-like, and light-hearted. I felt as if I was missing out. I would hear fabulous stories and sample yummy stateside treats provided by the other school children who would visit grandparents over the summer breaks and newly transferred students. My desire to see this magical land was relentless.

You may wonder how anyone would believe what they saw in television, movies, or magazines to be true? Let me explain. In the Philippines, the people on local television looked like people you would meet on the streets. The movies tend to be dramas about life of which I saw on (almost) a daily basis. The magazines showed Filipinos in real-life situations, and even though the models were pretty, they didn't look like store-bought dolls. From what I saw about America, it was a representation of what life was truly like.

In 1975, my dreams became a reality. My family was reassigned to Louisiana in the deep South of the United States. My airline flight was exhilarating! The stewardesses and pilots fit my expectations of real Americans: statuesque airline attendants, along with pilots who seemed to have perfectly chiseled features. I excused their lack of dancing and singing to the small space within the plane.

After we reached America, I distinctly remember being confused as to where all the border lines, state colors, blue water features and terrain features were as I gazed out the window to the America below. I didn't see one map feature below us. The lack of topographical features should have been an indication that my glamorized view of America would not be as expected. When we landed in Louisiana, my sister and I were sent to call our grandmother's house to let her know we arrived. This was another eye-opening adventure. In the Philippines, we had operators who monitor the phone lines. My sister picked up the phone handle, prepared to ask the operator to connect her to the number written on the piece of paper our mother had handed her. There was no voice, no assistance. Puzzled, we examined the phone booth, read the directions to insert a coin, and dialed our Grandmother's number.

The next befuddlement occurred as I gazed around the terminal to see hundreds of tired, disheveled, and agitated people scattered around a hot, dirty, and noisy airport. This was not the clean, bright, and shiny American experience I expected, and I still had not witnessed one group song or dance routine!

I discovered more misconceptions once we arrived at our grandmother's house and followed her into the kitchen. Grandma asked me to go to the freezer to get her an ingredient. When I opened it, I was astonished to discover it was a whole refrigerator devoted to leftovers! In the Philippines, there were no thoughts of storing food for months. Whatever was left over from one meal became part of the next meal.

America was quite different from life in the Philippines. As the days passed, I realized that what I saw and based my desire to come to America was based upon the Hollywood versions of life in America, not real life. Gradually, I learned to appreciate the less-than-idealistic version of what life was like in America. I saw similarities and many differences to the life I grew up knowing.

Experiencing life as an American in America was a fantastic learning experience. Within two years, my father's job returned our family to Clark Air Base, in the Philippines. My excitement and desire to return to the country I called home was based on the knowledge that although our little island country didn't have all the advantages and conveniences of American life, it was a less complicated and a happy way to live.

The lessons I learned during this point of my young life guided me into adulthood. Whenever I desired a particular standard of living, an experience, relationship, etc. I take the time to study, examine, and see the opportunity or experience from multiple points of views. Then, I ask myself: will I be disappointed if it does not meet my expectations? What will I do to adjust to the reality of the outcome? How will I react? Do I truly desire what I pursue, or can I adjust what I currently have?

A strong desire for something creates expectations of a "grass being greener" scenario. I learned that creating that image of what you want is beneficial. Just be sure to be prepared for what reality may bring. What I thought I wanted was bigger, brighter, and more. I learned to appreciate the simpler, laidback island life. Desire is based on what you don't have. You don't know what you've got until it's gone.

MICHELLE MRAS

About Michelle Mras: Michelle is an International TEDx Speaker, Communication Trainer, Success Coach, Co-Host of the Denim & Pearls podcast, the Author of Eat, Drink and Be Mary: A Glimpse Into a Life Well Lived and It's Not Luck: Overcoming You, and Host of the MentalShift show on The New Channel (TNC), Philippines.

Michelle is a survivor of multiple life challenges to include a traumatic brain injury and her current battle with breast cancer. She guides her clients to recognize the innate gifts within them, to stop apologizing for what they are not and step into who they truly are. She accomplishes this through one-on-one and group coaching, Training events, Keynote talks, her books, Podcasts and MentalShift television show.

Awarded the Inspirational Women of Excellence Award from the Women Economic Forum, New Delhi, India; the John Maxwell Team Culture Award for Positive Attitude, has been featured on hundreds of Podcasts, radio programs, several magazines, and lends her voice to audiobooks and has a habit of breaking out into song.

Michelle's driving thought is that every day is a gift. Tomorrow is never promised. Every moment is an opportunity to be the best version of you... Unapologetically,

Author's website: *www.MichelleMras.com*
Book Series Website & Author's Bio: *www.The13StepsToRiches.com*

Mickey Stewart

PIPING HOT DESIRE

One advantage of possessing a burning desire is that you feel so magnetically drawn to an idea while also maintaining a clear, confident KNOWING that it's already done. The disadvantage of possessing a burning desire…it often results in the people you love most questioning your mindset.

I was always a hopeless romantic, a dreamer who liked to fantasize about the future and get completely lost in my daydreams. Always being one to immerse myself in FEELING THE FEELINGS and living my dreams as if they had already happened, it shouldn't surprise me that I experienced my first burning desire when I was only sixteen.

Sitting in the backseat of our family's car, I made a remark about how grandiose my future was going to be—my husband, my career, my life. My statement was met with a silent, mutual smirk exchanged between my mom and older sister that spoke volumes.

"Just wait 'til she learns what life is REALLY like," followed by the comment, *"Well, I hope you plan to marry someone rich, then!"*

Looking back, I think my mom and sister may have felt sorry for me. They knew I still had a lot to learn, and they knew I was in for a rude awakening—that life was, *by no means,* a fairytale. Although the soft giggles echoing from the front seat weren't meant to hurt me, I later learned that this was the very beginning of a stream of comments both spoken and unspoken, that would continue to follow me, even to present day.

"That Mickey. Always a dreamer."

"At some point, she's going to need to GROW UP."

Although I was extremely naïve and nowhere near ready to have a boyfriend, their response to my ambitious proclamation would have caused most sixteen-year-olds to question themselves, to question their dreams. But, strangely enough, the opposite thing happened to me that day: a flame was ignited so deep within my soul that it fueled an incredibly confident retort that surprised even me, for I don't think I even had the thought until that exact moment when the words began pouring out of my mouth.

"I'm going to marry a cute, young, Scottish piper with a strong Scottish last name.

But he has to be a really good piper – like world-class."

I would go on to repeat these exact words throughout my teens and early twenties, whenever the topic of boyfriends or husbands arose. I would later learn this was my first encounter with a burning desire— because, the minute I said these words... in MY mind... they were already true.

Fast forward seven years later to the early summer of 1994. At the age of twenty-three, I found myself in Halifax, Nova Scotia, where some of my bagpiping and drumming friends were participating in the critically acclaimed Nova Scotia International Tattoo, a week-long event featuring bagpipes, drums, bands, dancers, and acrobats. One of the organizers, who was also a good friend of mine, handed me a ticket that would change my life forever. This ticket came in the form of a press pass, providing me backstage access to the entire event, which meant I could attend every single performance, including the afterparties!

Providing me this pass was my friend's way of ensuring the visiting performers would experience a truly Nova Scotian good time. You see, I'm known for my ability for getting parties started by breaking out my bodhrán drum and getting the tunes going. That, coupled with the fact that I'm *always* the last one standing, would provide plenty of reasons for people to participate in the afterparties until the sun came up (which, in Nova Scotia, is our measuring stick for how good a party really is). So, as not to disappoint, I agreed to bring my bodhrán, my enthusiasm, and my love of music to these social gatherings.

So, it all began on this one particular evening, the night at the final cast party. A band that was performing was about to take a break when one of the organizers approached another performer and said, "There's this girl from Cape Breton with her bodhrán. Would you get up and play with her during the band's intermission?"

He said, "Sure."

Then, the same gent came over to me and said, "There's this guy from Scotland with his smallpipes. Would you get up and play with him during intermission?"

And I said, "Yes."

When the band finished performing, I walked onto the stage and found myself face to face with a cute, young, Scottish piper. There we were, just the two of us, on this huge rectangular stage, with hundreds of sets of eyes fixated on us. Had we had an opportunity to discuss the selection of tunes we should play? No. Did we have a chance to practice? No. Should we have been nervous? Perhaps. Was I nervous? ABSOLUTELY NOT!

So, the cute, young, Scottish piper looked at me and asked, "What would you like to play?"

To which I responded, "You just play whatever and I'll follow you."

To this day, I don't believe we even knew each other's names until we were introduced to the audience. His name was Mark! And the very minute Mark started piping, I was in love. While I realize it sounds cliché, I truly felt as if my entire body was literally struck by lightning, and I knew instantly he was THE ONE.

Upon returning home that evening, I found myself bursting with excitement to tell my roommates about this amazing encounter I had with the cute, young, Scottish piper. Within minutes of sharing my story, one of my roommates, who is extremely intuitive, gasped and boldly exclaimed, *"Oh my God! You're totally going to marry this guy!"*

After experiencing a grand total of three first dates throughout my entire life (which, I must add, never resulted in a second date), I responded, "Yes, Karen. Yes, I will."

I, Mickey Pero, had met my cute, young, Scottish piper that I was to marry.

Three days after meeting Mark, his pipe band travelled to Cape Breton, Nova Scotia, where they were to perform at the Gaelic College, which was located just minutes away from my family home. I made the four-hour journey from Halifax to Cape Breton to see Mark, and we ended up talking until the wee hours of the morning. We were both so incredibly shy that we didn't even dare sneak a first kiss. But, as I drove over Kelly's Mountain at three o'clock in the morning to my family home, I decided right then and there that I had to go to Scotland to see how Mark felt about me. After all, since we were going to be married, it would be best to find out if the guy even liked me.

After seven years of my burning desire appearing to lay dormant, a new 'spark' was ignited from the happenings of the past week. It was finally time to set my plans into motion! As a young university student who was basically surviving from paycheck to paycheck (with no savings), my first priority was to muster up enough money to get to Scotland.

So, on Monday morning, after climbing three flights of stairs to my boss's office, I informed him that I was going to Scotland, that I needed a few weeks off (in the middle of the peak tourist season), and that I was planning to attend the World Pipe Band Championships. In truth, I was traveling those 4,267 miles to find out how my cute, young, Scottish bagpiper felt about me. Regardless of my boss's response, I *was* going to Scotland.

My burning desire continued to WOW me! Not only was I able to convince my boss to grant me the time off that I needed, but I also managed to persuade him to give me a pay advance.

Later that day, sitting on the living room floor of the condo I shared with my roommates, I found myself becoming increasingly excited while rolling some loose change they gave me. With my plane tickets now in hand (thanks to the advance in my paycheck), I needed to find enough money to cover my other expenses. But how?

The answer came quickly.

Although I'm a skilled drummer, I could also play the bagpipes! So, after borrowing a set of pipes from a friend, I went to the Halifax waterfront for an afternoon of busking. Now, I was closer to having a bed to sleep in when I arrived in Scotland.

Before I knew it, my extremely shy, never-had-a-boyfriend, mousy self was phoning this cute, young, guy in Scotland to notify him that "I'm coming over to see you!"

Five months after that trip to Scotland, I was living there. And, after twenty-four years of marriage, we are still like two young kids in love.

When you possess a true burning desire, obstacles that initially look impossible to overcome magically transform into mere bends in the road.

My friends and family now witness me living my fairytale life with my handsome, world-renowned musician and composer husband—who just so happens to have a strong Scottish last name. Added bonus - we get to attend a ball at a castle every year!

Looking back now, I don't believe I have yet to meet another person that has displayed as much determination as that twenty-three-year-old version of myself. And I can't tell you how often I wished I could have "bottled" the burning desire I first experienced sitting in the back seat of our family car—so that I could sneak a sip of it every time I feel my confidence waver…which it does…quite frequently.

To this day, I realize I still give my family reason to often question my mindset, and that's completely fine with me. After all, it was their not-so-positive response to my initial grand proclamation that triggered my burning desire in the first place.

MICKEY STEWART

About Mickey Stewart: Born in Cape Breton, Canada, Mickey Stewart is a musician, coach, and author who has been a player and instructor of the snare drum and bodhrán for forty years.

Responsible for heading up the drum program at Ardvreck School in Perthshire, Scotland since 2002, Mickey is in high demand to teach throughout the U.K. and North America.

Creator and founder of BodhránExpert.com, her YouTube videos have received more than two million views from students and fans from every country throughout the world.

Over the past eight years, she's been involved in the TV and film industry as a supporting artist. Even more recently, she's begun following her newest passion, which is teaching others how to share their talents with the world.

Stewart lives in Crieff, Scotland with her husband of twenty-four years, Scottish musician and composer Mark Stewart, along with their 16-year-old son, Cameron, who is also a piper.

Author's website: *www.MickeyStewart.com*
Book Series Website & Author's Bio: *www.The13StepsToRiches.com*

MAGICAL ALIGNMENT

I am a UCSD (University of California San Diego) writing teacher for a course called "The Pursuit of Happiness" and a Conscious Communication consultant. Every year, I get to teach 100 students about how to feel happier by learning how to consciously communicate with themselves and others, and in the business world, I get to teach the same content to start-up entrepreneurs, business owners, and corporate executives. I help people find more happiness by helping them navigate all of their communication situations in every area of their life.

Since I teach a course called "The Pursuit of Happiness," people often ask me how they can feel happier, and I explain it like this. Your level of happiness is determined by the quality of your relationship to yourself and to others. The quality of your relationships is determined by the quality of your communication with yourself and others. Communication is the foundation of every relationship and every moment in time. It is the root of every happy moment and every moment of frustration in your life. When you fix your communication skills, you fix just about everything else in your life, too. It is the single most important key to happiness. It is the single most important concept to learn, explore, and master. And it is the single most important way to transform everything in your life.

In both the classroom and the boardroom, I tell people that feeling happier starts with knowing how to communicate with yourself first. Communicating with yourself about your own desires and learning how to attract those desires into your life is one of the most important skills to learn and hone in order to experience the life you've always dreamed of living.

When a client first comes to me, they are generally experiencing what I call a "Cocoon Moment." As you can probably guess, this phrase lends itself to the caterpillar/butterfly metaphor, and it indicates a dark, dreary, uncomfortable moment in a person's life that feels scary, stressful, and uncomfortable, but one they will eventually transmute into a positive transformative experience. In these moments, people often complain that their needs and wants have not been met in some big way, and they are dissatisfied with how their life currently looks. They are primarily living in a state where their fear-based emotions—like disappointment, regret, or frustration—are dominating their thoughts and actions, and they cannot see how to start creating the life they want to live again. People come to me because they know they are in a dark place and they want to shift, but what they don't know is they are really just having a cocoon moment, and they will soon transform into a different, more empowered version of themselves. I kindly assure them that "this is just a moment in time," and then, I guide them through our first exercise, which I will share with you below, called "The Sentence Swap."

This exercise teaches people a simple way to gain clarity around what they desire, and it also teaches how to write, speak, and feel this desire into existence in the most efficient and effective way. The problem that most people face is not that their needs and wants are going unfulfilled, but that they have not transformed their needs and wants into desires.

The important concept to understand here is that words carry energy. Every thought, feeling, action, and desire starts with the words we are using to communicate with ourselves and with others. We must be careful with the words we use, because they shape our reality. Certain words hold a negative charge, while other words hold a positive charge. The words "needs" and "wants" are lower vibrational words. They are disempowering, and they make us sound needy and feel that way, too. Your wants and needs are tired of being spoken about. They are old, fear-based thoughts that you've likely complained about many times to many people, and they ultimately just express lack in your life. We all know what our needs and wants are, but we often do not give ourselves the opportunity to think about our true desires. For some people, even saying the word "desire" makes us blush, as we often relegate this word to the area of our life that has to do with sex and passion. While it certainly deserves its place in that area, it also warrants a place to be used as a verb in every other area of our lives, too.

Try this out:

I really need a bigger house *versus* I desire a bigger house.

I really need a new job *versus* I desire a new job.

I want a new car *versus* I desire a new car.

I want a relationship *versus* I desire a relationship.

Can you feel the difference when you say these sentences? Can you feel how the first version sounds kind of needy and heavy, and the second one sounds lighter and more fun? Talking about our desires can be playful and pleasurable. It leaves space for our imagination to stretch beyond the limits and barriers that our old needs and wants hold. This little shift in language can make a very big impact on how you create your reality.

Now, let's get to "The Sentence Swap" exercise.

Take out a piece of paper and write down a list of all of your current needs and wants. Write them down like fill-in-the-blank sentences.

Write "I need…" "I want…" and try to write at least ten for each one. I encourage my clients to set a timer for two to three minutes and try to write as much as they can without stopping and without picking up their pen from the paper. This is called "Stream of Consciousness Writing" or "Automatic Writing," and it helps to allow your unconscious to speak to you. You can learn a lot about yourself and your needs/wants when you allow yourself to freely write without any judgement or correction.

After you have completed the first list, I want you to rewrite both lists and replace "I want" and "I need" with "I desire" for every single sentence. After that list is complete, read the new sentences out loud and feel the difference. The second version will likely feel lighter, more fun, and more pleasurable to read. You will probably even catch yourself smiling a bit as you read this version. If you want to take your manifesting skills to the next level, remember that space for a minute. Read them again if you need to, and feel how it feels in your body to read something that lights you up.

When you read about one of your favorite desires, the one you'd be most excited about, where do you feel it? Is it in your heart, in your smile, in your gut? Sit and breathe into the space for a little bit and really feel that feeling. We create with our thoughts, our speech, and our feelings. Emotion is the most powerful force, and you create quickly when your thoughts, your speech, and your feelings are all in alignment. Challenge yourself to stay in this mode of speaking about your desires, instead of your needs/wants. When you catch yourself saying, "I want…", stop yourself, and replace it with "I desire…" Stay consistent with this.

Train yourself to do this sentence swap until it becomes natural for you to speak about your desires first. It will take time to get acclimated to this new way of speaking, but eventually, you will get used to it. And bring it all together by thinking about what you want, speaking about what you want, and feeling what it feels like to have what you want, and you will begin to see how those desires start to show up in your reality in beautiful, synchronistic ways that often feel magical and totally in alignment.

NATALIE SUSI

About Natalie Susi: Natalie has more than 14 years of experience as a teacher, speaker, entrepreneur and mentor. Currently she's a 5-year UCSD professor focusing on communications and the Pursuit of Happiness. As an entrepreneur, she founded and grew Bare Organic Mixers beverage company for 8 years resulting in an acquisition in 2014.

After selling the company, Natalie combined her educational background as a teacher and her experience as an entrepreneur to provide personal development coaching and consulting to individuals, businesses, and creative entrepreneurs. She developed a program called Conscious Conversations and utilizes a step-by-step process called The Alignment Method to support leaders in cultivating conscious teams and businesses through a process of self-reflection, self-discovery, and self-ascension that ultimately increases profits, productivity, and the growth of the individuals personally and professionally.

Author's website: *www.NatalieSusi.com*
Book Series Website & Author's Bio: *www.The13StepsToRiches.com*

LE LOUVRE IS LE LIMIT

To manifest your desire, set an intention, take action, and receive.

It was December of 2017, and I was flipping through a magazine as I came across beautiful pictures of the iconic museums, the Tate (London) and Le Louvre (Paris). Something possessed me to cut out the two images as I thought to myself, *Wouldn't it be cool to have my art in there some day?* It was a faint thought that I never paid attention to until I received a call from a gallery one day in May of 2018.

It was a gallery that had seen my work earlier in the year in New York. They told me they loved my work, wanted to represent me, and asked if I was interested in showing in the fall in Torino, Italy. My immediate thought was, *Torino? But I love Paris!*

So, I confidently approached the thought and asked, "What about Paris?"

They said, "Oh yes, we're stopping in Paris as well, but we felt you would prefer to show in Italy."

"Why would you think that?" I asked. There was a dialogue going on in my head simultaneously about how they knew nothing about me, how dare they judge me and assume where I want to show my work.

The kind gentleman on the phone responded, "Your work is refined, and we met you in New York. You may not remember, but the impression you gave off about yourself was rather elevated."

My inner dialogue continued, *Oh! Right, people are watching everything, all the time. Thank God I made a good impression. Wait... good thing I was being true to myself.* My mind got a little distracted as a ton of thoughts came at me about why personal presence is so important. It validated everything about my decision to write my book *Boss Vibes - Self-Esteem, Success, and the Art of Etiquette.*

"So, what do you think? We can show your work in October," he said.

As he named off a few galleries, I asked, "What about museums? Can you get my work into a museum?"

There was a long silence after my question. I held my breath as I started beating myself up—*why couldn't you just take what they offered, why did you have to ask for more? Make a joke and say— Just kidding!*

Suddenly the voice on the line came back and hesitantly responded, "Well....if you're willing to wait a few weeks, we can show your work in the Louvre."

Wait, did I hear that right? The Louvre? As in *the* iconic museum of the world in Paris, Le Louvre? But I was embarrassed to confirm. I held my breath and said, "Yes!" Within that ten-minute conversation, my art career went from national to global!

Where did this start? I was flying home on a Sunday from Miami to Dallas. I received an email that morning that someone dropped out from the one of the biggest art fairs in the country, New York Art Expo, and I could take their booth. The show started on Thursday. It was the most exciting opportunity at that moment; however, I was also working a full-time job, I was a high school band mom, and I had so many other responsibilities.

I would have to arrange for everything in less than a day. I would have to get home, buy packing materials, pack all my artwork, and get on a flight to New York on Wednesday to be ready for the opening by Thursday. I had no team, no help, I was a one (wo-) man show. It was a solopreneur moment at its best. I had forty-eight hours to prepare for a show I had no clue was coming my way. THIS was a moment for me to receive. To say "yes," instead of, "but how?" And I did. I said yes, and this yes was a snowball effect for me. The more I said "yes," the more doors opened for me.

It was no joke doing an art show all by yourself for the very first time. I was running all over Manhattan looking for tape, nails, hammer and 3M strips to secure the art on the walls. The Uber driver wasn't allowed to park anywhere, and I had to take eight large pieces of art and my luggage a quarter of a mile to my booth. Working your own art fair means standing on your feet twelve hours a day, all dressed up, with a smile on your face, repeating your story to thousands of people who walked by, some with genuine interest, while others are only pretending to be curious about your work, because they really want to see what your neighbors have— and worse, solicitors who wanted to work a deal. It's New York; you must expect it all!

I typically didn't attend all my shows. It was nearly impossible. Especially that year. I did twelve shows in eight months that year while prioritizing my responsibilities as a high school band mom. If you're not familiar with that role, it's 6 a.m. practices and games that end at midnight the entire fall season, followed by concert season and competitions in the spring. But this show was different. Paris was my favorite place; how could I not go? So, we went! Yes, my son went with us. It was about maintaining my commitments *and* receiving. It's possible to do both when your intentions are pure, and you are authentic to yourself.

People showed up in 18th century ball gowns on the opening night of the show in Paris. It was spectacular.

Learning to receive is an ongoing process. It starts with saying "yes" with lots of action in between. It starts with genuinely letting all the excuses go of why you can't do something. We've mastered that art for so long, it's natural to first think of why we can't do something or why something won't work. In the receiving process, we must release all excuses.

Remember, we are divine beings. We are spiritual beings having a human experience. God, the Universe, a higher power, whatever words you wish to call it— that power is within us. It's simple, but we tend to complicate it with our minds. We over-analyze the "how" and quickly lose sight of our dreams. When we do this, we're disrespecting that higher power within us. The same higher power that makes the Universe function precisely the way it does. So, how can it not work for us?

Release all the thoughts of "how" and "what if." Say "yes" to everything that's in alignment with you and your dreams, and take inspired action towards it. That's when you'll start to receive.

The starting point to my journey was setting an intention. It took me some time to learn how to receive. But when I learned how, I ended up having more art shows that year than I ever imagined. My work was shown at museums and galleries in Paris, Torino, the Hamptons, New York City, Miami, and Dallas. It was all unexpected. It was all from taking inspired action towards my intention and saying "yes" to everything that was in alignment with my dreams. It's never easy, but it's simple. There's a formula or system for everything in life, and my formula is to set an intention, take inspired action, and receive.

In life, you end up where you only imagined.

NITA PATEL

About Nita Patel: Nita is a Best-Selling Author, speaker, and artist who believes in modern etiquette as a path to becoming our best selves.

Through her professional years, Ms. Patel has 25 years of demonstrated technology leadership experience in various industries specifically with a concentrated focus in health care for 14 of those 20+ years. She's shown her art across the world to include the Louvre in Paris. She's a best-selling author and performance coach, pursuing her master's in industrial organizational (I-O) psychology at Harvard. Her investment in psychology theory and practice is what led her to a deep interest in helping others. She has become deeply and passionately devoted to nurturing others and in building their confidence and brand through speaking and consultative practices.

Author's website: *www.Nita-Patel.com*
Book Series Website & Author's Bio: *www.The13StepsToRiches.com*

Olga Geidane

DESIRE FOR PEOPLE AND PEOPLE FOR DESIRE

Think of someone you desired more than anything. Do you remember how much you wanted that person to be next to you? You wanted to spend time with them, touch them, and smell them.

The truth is, when you desire someone, you will do anything and everything to make things happen. You will fly across the ocean to spend a weekend with them and will stay awake late at night, sacrificing your sleep, just so you can talk to them a little bit more, despite your mind telling you off.

When you are passionate about someone, you ignore your mind chatter. You never know how things will end, and yet, you are ready to risk it all. And here is the most exciting thing: when you follow your instincts and your heart in these situations, miraculously, everything falls in place and aligns together.

If you are like me, then you followed your passionate love, and things did not work out, yet you always can say that at least you learned something. All of those lessons made you and me who we are now. Others will say that *they followed their crazy desires in their hearts,* and they are still happy with that person, maybe even three decades later. And this is very interesting when it comes to love; we always say the same thing across the world: **follow your heart!**

But when it comes to our life desires, goals, and dreams, we become very logical, pragmatical, strategic, and we stay in our minds 100 percent. Then, we want to know about the result before we even make a move. How strange is that? Why would we follow our desires in our love life and switch to logic when it comes to other passions in life?

What is sexual desire? It is an accumulation of sexual energy *within your body and mind (your brain creates everything!)* that blinds the logical sense when it becomes too strong. In a moment of passion, you are unstoppable, and your mind is uncontrollable. It is one of the highest motivational states. You are ready to do anything to fulfill your wants, and nothing can stop you, right? And you get satisfied after you get what you wanted.

So, what happens to your desires in life? Why are people generally a lot less motivated, committed, and driven than within sexual desires when it comes to accomplishments and achievements? The answer is in the difference in dopamine levels in both scenarios. When you fulfill your *intimate fantasies,* you release *dopamine.* Dopamine is responsible for feeling good, joy, and satisfaction and desire, and motivation. The logical part switches off after sex.

That feeling is very addictive. The more driven a person you are in life, the higher the sexual desire you will have. After working with thousands of high achievers, leaders of organizations, and sportspeople, I can confirm that this is true.

Let's look at allowing yourself to experience the same level of dopamine release when it comes to accomplishing your goals. If you are just like most people, then once you have achieved something, you move on without celebrating or acknowledging your win.

Subconsciously, you are not hugely motivated to go after what you want because, at the end of the day, "there will be no fun and no pleasure" after your victory. Since you were little, you were most likely programmed to not shout out loud about your achievements, which means you don't even allow the dopamine level to build up!

Can we change that?

The good news is that you are not a tree, and you *can* change your program. Even trees find ways to grow better and more robust, so what can stop you? Nothing can stop you when you commit to your desire like a parent commits to their baby. Perhaps, you wonder how parental commitment connects with a desire?

A DESIRE to co-create a unique human being, to leave something and someone vital after you, to continue the family clan—that is what drives most men and women to have children.

When a woman decides to become a mother, she *knows* that there will be around forty weeks of pregnancy—which could go wrong. There could also be a very long and challenging labor. There will be sleepless nights for at least a few years, dealing with tantrums, and later on, come challenges of a teenage stage. And yet, *no mother on Earth will ever refuse to have a baby when she FEELS like having one.* When she faces challenges on her way, she is so determined to get pregnant that she will do *anything* and will pay *any price* to make it happen.

Following your desires is best compared to the process of pregnancy and parenting. Whether you are a parent or not, it doesn't matter, as you will be able to relate to these five lessons. If you apply these tips in your life towards your desires, you will be experiencing many higher levels of joy and satisfaction when you will be achieving your goals!

1. **Follow your feelings and your desires—they are always on time!** If you have a DESIRE to do, accomplish, create something right this moment—that's because right now is a PERFECT TIME! Your *desire comes at the peak of your capabilities to make your dream a reality!* If you observe when a woman gets pregnant with ease, usually it is at the height of her excellent health. **You have the desire at the right time**, so use the energy and the drive towards accomplishing it!

2. **Be patient and trust all the processes happening at the right time.** Just like a pregnant woman sometimes gets tired of pregnancy and even has some complications, she *knows* that the baby will be born when the timing is right. She might want the baby sooner, but she knows that particular body parts are developing at certain times, and if you speed up the process of birth, the baby will be delivered prematurely. In my case, I wanted my son to be born on the

5th of February—after all of my exams at the university. As you can imagine, my plan didn't work out! Every process takes time, and you have to master patience. Once you learn how to trust the process, you will have to take another step towards your goal.

3. **Commit to your desire, despite not knowing how** like a loving parent commits to their baby without a manual on raising a perfect human being. Don't we all wish to have a step-by-step guide as a parent? Yet, each of us can write one ourselves once we have raised our children. You will never become perfect enough, ready enough, or confident enough. Embrace the unknown. Remember that this is what excites you when you desire someone intimately!

4. **Be relentlessly innovative, allow yourself to be creative, and come up with new ways.** A loving parent is very creative with educating their child, how they prepare them for life, and how they entertain them. If one method doesn't work, a parent will always find another way, whether it is how to feed a child broccoli or teach them how to count to ten.

5. **CELEBRATE.** *This* is the most crucial step! Think of parents seeing a child taking their first steps and then falling. Can you imagine one of them scrutinizing that child who just fell, saying that they will never walk because they failed? NO! It just doesn't happen! Quite the opposite: parents are celebrating EVERY LITTLE step, because this way, their accomplishments increase the level of joy and happiness in you! It's time to allow yourself to celebrate your little wins when your small and big desires get fulfilled in life.

By applying these five straightforward tips in your life, you will retrain and reprogram your brain to receive more joy from achieving in life, not just in your love life and sex life.

And lastly, what if something goes wrong when you follow your desire and passion? That is the most common question I receive, and indeed that was the question I was asking myself, too! Think: what is the worst that can happen when you follow your desires? You will get experience, and you will learn. You will be transformed; you will never be the same person again.

A much better question is: What will happen *if you choose not* to follow your desire? Then, you will *never* find out how your life would change, what impact you would leave, how much happier you could be, and what wonders of life you would discover.

So, follow your desires in life with the persistence of a parent and a passion of a lover. Then, you will break through ANYTHING!

OLGA GEIDANE

About Olga Geidane: Olga is an Executive Mindset and Performance Coach, International Speaker, a Best-Selling Author, and a Regional President of the Professional Speaking Association. She is a host of Olga's Show and A World-Traveler. "Change your mindset = change your life" is Olga's favorite quote and she truly walks her talk: being a divorcee and a single mom at the age of 24, she came to the UK from Latvia with no spoken English, just £100 in her pocket and a 2.5-year-old son. Her success in life is based on continuous growth and transformation of her mindset and habits.

Being an expert in mindset transformation, Olga knows how to challenge and press the right buttons in order to achieve the best results for her clients. Her non-judgmental and confidential approach helps people to dive deeper into the darkest alleys of their minds whilst being supported and walked through the journey by Olga not only during the coaching/advisory sessions but also in between them. She will not only elevate you but also transform you and will help you to live the life you desire!

Author's website: *www.OlgaGeidane.com*
Book Series Website & Author's Bio: *www.The13StepsToRiches.com*

Paul Andrés

WHAT WE FIGHT FOR

"Following your heart's desire will lead you in
the direction your spirit wants to go."
-Oprah Winfrey

There have been many times in my life where I have felt lost, alone, or forgotten. I took a wrong turn, made a poor decision, or trusted the words of others who were, in fact, not my friends. I would often fall, wallowing in all of my struggle and shortcomings. And occasionally, I would find myself on the grips of what felt like utter and complete failure. But with every downfall, there is a choice. The choice to continue or not to continue. And for some reason, whenever it came to choosing between defeat or the pain to continue on, the choice to continue on always seemed to be made for me.

There is a flame deep within my soul that has burned for lifetimes. A sleeping ember that ignites me into action, even when nothing but failure is here to face me. Different from want or need, this flame holds much more power. It seems to know where I come from and where I am meant to go. Always igniting the fight to move forward, the urge to go on and the will to survive. And while for years, I didn't know what it was that made me pick myself up or take another step, I have finally come to learn exactly what it's called. Desire. My heart's desire, to be precise.

Whenever I find myself in the epicenter of my struggle, there is always a moment of stillness, where I am surrounded by darkness somewhere deep within my mind, listening to the world still happening outside me. It is just before I decide to make the choice to give up or give in to my struggle, when the noise outside will slowly begin to subside. And ever so lightly, out of the darkness that surrounds me, I will begin to see a faint outline of two people. Hard to see at first, but slowly, they reveal themselves. One with kind eyes and labored hands of purpose, the other always smelling of rose petals and flowers, but with a smile that unexplainably soothes your soul to comfort. My grandparents, Fernando and Guadalupe Ortiz—or Apa and Ama, as we would call them—are the very two who are responsible for gifting me my flame.

As I begin to see them both clearer and clearer, a peaceful quiet overcomes me, and in an instant, I see their lives and the journey they made for everyone who came after them. In the dawn of 1940, in the small border town of Elsa, Texas, their journeys began. My grandma, a young Mexican girl of thirteen, with light skin and wavy, dark hair, worked in the kitchen of an expansive ranch with her mother. Every day, the ranch owner would task them with feeding two meals to over thirty Mexican immigrant workers. It was grueling work, but something she had become accustomed to from a very young age. Being a girl of Mexican descent who spoke no English meant school was not an option. So, taking on some of the burden her mother carried became her responsibility. So, she helped cook and clean every day, for much of her childhood.

One spring, a new batch of Mexican immigrants arrived to work on the ranch. In the group was a chestnut-colored young man, who always seemed to be smiling. He arrived with two of his brothers. He was not loud or pretending to be much like many other young men. He was kind, light-hearted, and very hard-working. Always being recognized as one of the top workers, which made it impossible for that young girl in the kitchen to not notice him. Over the course of a year, they let smiles and stolen glances do all the talking, until one day, the young man asked the young girl's father for her hand in marriage. On September 21, 1941, the two were married on the same ranch where they lived and worked. Within their first year of marriage, at the age of fourteen, my grandma had their first child. And over the next fifteen or so years, they would learn to become true partners in marriage, welcome eleven more children into the world, say goodbye to one at the age of three, and survive constant racial discrimination and societal mistreatment, all while living in a small ten-by-ten shack, with no running water or bathroom, courtesy of the ranch owner.

During their time on the ranch as a family, things became increasingly harder. Being Mexican immigrants who spoke little to no English, with no real education, limited their options and possibilities. It was during this time that our flame of desire was ignited and cultivated. With every idea to make a better life for themselves and children, came a list of reasons and realities to face why it wouldn't work. They began to realize that being farmworkers and immigrants in Texas meant that their children's dreams and hopes were limited to that of their parents. The social outlook was very much that in the south, and Mexican immigrants experienced much of the harsh realities of Jim Crow America.

With the flame of desire growing strong and stronger within them and the reality of life on the farm being so limited, they made a bold and risky move. They allowed their hearts' desire for a better future for their family to drive them into action. They had heard of farm work in the north, where people of color and immigrants alike were treated humanely. They were given living wages, options for available healthcare, and even assistance with housing. In the mid-1950s, with less than $100 dollars to their name, eleven children to care for, and both knowing little to no English, they decided to leave the ranch behind and relocate to Washington state. They found a small home in the Yakima Valley, where my grandma made every meal from scratch, raised her children and many of her children's children—including me, and constantly held family get-togethers and parties. My grandpa found work immediately, working on a hop farm for a very just and kind farm owner, and spent his weekends humming to himself while rocking on the front porch or tending to his yard, where he grew beautiful rose bushes for my grandma and delicious herbs and vegetables for his family, like strawberries, pumpkins, tomatoes, and basil.

Their entire life and journey is shown to me in an instant, and every time, it helps to remind me to appreciate their gift of my flame. Learning how their hearts' desire pushed them through dark days and unbeatable odds, to create the family that I know and love today is always awe-inspiring. And to know that level of desire burns inside of me is nothing short of humbling. It is because of their desire for more that I am here today. They are responsible for every opportunity and every choice I have been given. Their desire made it possible for me to graduate high school and earn a college degree, to open my businesses, to own a home, to fight for my right to marry my husband, and fight even harder to adopt my son. Their memories will live inside of me forever, and it's their gift, the flight that is my heart's desire, that I, too, hope to pass onto my son, so he, too, can desire the life of his dreams.

My Thank You to Apa and Ama

I hear the music of trumpets roaring

to the Cumbia beats of plucked guitar strings.

Loud gritos punctuate every verse,

leaping through staccato melodies that fill the air of

hills and valleys with excitement that lingers for a lifetime.

I smell fresh flour tortillas

warming on the heavy hum of the hot comal

as refried beans simmer sizzling with a savory decadence

only real Manteca can make,

while the mouthwatering smokiness of barbacoa,

dances through the air, effortlessly finding the rhythm.

I see mouths laughing and telling stories of past beginnings

between cracks in the faux mahogany-planked walls,

arms extend and embrace atop sofas made of crushed velvet,
speckled with imprinted images of

wheelbarrows in flower fields faded by time.

while feet dance furiously on the oil-stained driveway,

expertly maneuvering across the embossed remnants
from parties long forgotten and celebrations yet to be had.

and always . . .
just as the memory begins to blur around the edges,
a signal that my time must soon come to an end,
I find myself alone inside their quaint home.
always safe and forever wanted,
engulfed by a peaceful quiet
where across a valley of taught green carpet,
almond eyes full of purpose and endless hope
stare back at me.
scattered across glistening walls
between holy relics and whispered secrets.
Weathered by circumstance and time,
they sit patiently inside frames of captured moments,
offering wordless stories, countless dreams, and endless lessons
with each gaze met. It's always then, at that moment
that goodbyes are shared in silence, but loud with knowing,
and in an instant, I return to what is.

My life now,where I hold tightly near my heart

these memories of my familia.

A family full of life.

that showed me what it is to dream,

how it feels to be loved,

and what it takes to not be forgotten.

By: Paul Andrés

PAUL ANDRÉS

About Paul Andrés: Paul is an award-winning conscious entrepreneur, visual storyteller, and intuitive coach. From digital and interior design, to business clarity and personal growth coaching, to social justice advocacy and volunteering, Paul is proof that aligning your passions with your purpose is the true magic to success. He currently devotes his time to helping awakened entrepreneurs and heart-centered creatives design the life they deserve through personal and professional coaching and consulting, as well as shedding light on uncomfortable topics that bring awareness to the social justice issues of today as the host of his video podcast, Your Mind. Paul is also a two-time #1 Best-Selling Author. You can catch him as a featured guest speaker at events across the country.

"Home is so many things, but ultimately, it's where life happens. It's where we sleep and grow a family, it's where we play and grow professionally, and it's where we learn and grow within. Each home plays a key role in helping us design a whole life—the life we all deserve."

— Paul Andrés

Author's website: *www.PaulAndres.com*
Book Series Website & Author's Bio: *www.The13StepsToRiches.com*

Paul Capozio

BARNES HAD NO "PLAN B"

When we speak of desire, many of us have experienced that deep burning. A feeling that is most recognizable when it hits us. It's similar to its cousin, the survival instinct, always there just beneath the surface, an involuntary reflex.

This type of desire is brought on by fantasy, dream building, visual stimulation, physical attraction, even jealousy. In the case of our survival instinct, it is brought on by outside stimuli. We have all heard stories mothers lifting cars off of their babies. The ability for the most introverted to muster not only the courage, but the negotiating skills to ask for money for the last bus leaving for home at 3 a.m. because of a lost wallet.

The issue here is that when we talk of desire, it is rarely in the pursuit of success. The most common example given when asked is that of sexual desire. It is rare when people think of the desire of a Tesla—I'm referring to the man, not the ownership of the car.

To be more direct, the area of desire of business success, that desire is not instinctive for most. So, if it stands that we can manifest sexual desire, or desire for money—which can sometimes disguise itself as pure greed—how do we then develop a desire for work ethic and sheer stick-to-it-iveness.

Good news: it's possible!

We must search for the feelings within ourselves, that tiny spark of desire, and then, fan the flames. Allow me to show examples of those sparks and what they feel like so you can recognize them easily when they happen. You already have the chemistry inside you, you're just feeling it for someone else's success.

A great example is what we feel when meeting a great rock star or sports star. How effortlessly we can cheer them on and get nervous excitement about meeting them and thinking of what they have achieved. Think about the old film clips of the Beatles; they always show cuts of screaming and crying girls in the audience. All that expression in a time when those feelings were just not out front like that! It was enough for them to do, say, and think things never felt before for many of them. Desire—not just sexual; it was deeper than that.

We don't question having an emotional and visceral response when we have front row seats. We all have desire and drive, the only issue is in many cases, it's not for us; it's for someone else. That is because it takes much less commitment on our part.

The big issue is the successes of celebrities we get excited about shows some laziness on our part. The work is not required by us; it only requires us to admire it. That is why people love pro sports so much, and recliners are now sold in rows of three as home theater chairs! "Come, friends, and feel with me the success of others.

Make me feel better that I'm not the only one in love with someone else's success all from the comfort of this easy chair."

This admiration, desire, and appreciation will even allow us to look beyond negative feelings, which is how bad decisions are made or bad partnerships. That is how powerful desire is. Take the case of Michael Jackson, an amazing talent. A singer, dancer, writer, and performer, his talent was without question. An amazing fan base so loyal that, regardless of allegations, had unwavering devotion. Now, I do not bring this up to voice an opinion. I only bring this out to show how desire and appreciation affects us so deeply. You see, we all regularly experience desire and drive. The only issue is it's not for us; it's for someone else, even when that desire manifests sexually.

A teenager having the wherewithal to buy a twelve-hundred-dollar smartphone proves sheer desire. That instinctual drive shows the ability, yet sadly, it ends there for most, as we cannot translate that desire when the dream is not big enough or seems unattainable. I can go on and on here about society's role in all of this. The dream and desire suppression is out there hitting us in the face every day, but let's face it: those are just excuses. The point is desire is so often born out of desperation to take hold. So many success stories start with, "So, there I was at rock bottom, broke, hungry, and alone." Well, fear not, it does not have to come to that, but you see, you need a powerful reason to have true desire, and some will need that devastation to make it strong enough. Hope and and willpower alone will not get it done.

Desire will build best in its seedling form. That is called goal-setting. Goals help you build to a fever pitch and borderline obsession. Then **go for obsession!**

I like having three levels to each goal.

Level 1 goal-setting needs to be a relatively easily achievable goal—a warm-up. This provides positive feedback and mindset; you must make a mark in the win column right away. So, if your true goal is to land that big account, your level one goal is to develop a personal relationship with the person who can land you the interview! That will be a personal growth stimulator. You cannot build desire without positive feedback.

Level 2 goal-setting needs to be your actual goal for that timeframe or other metric. I cannot give you specifics without a coaching session, but this is it. It's game day! So, if that big account is a one-million-dollar sales ticket, well, your ducks should be all in a row, and you better have been manifesting this from your deep-seated desire for it!

Level 3 goal-setting needs to be outside your comfort zone and over and above your level 2 goal. This is sheer desire—nothing more. You need to shoot past your level 2 as far as you can. In the case of our one-million-dollar sales example, offer them the possibility above and beyond their request! Would they appreciate a better deal if they took two or even three million dollars of your product or service to create more value to our buyer?

In the worst case, the reason you miss it is they do not see the value, or your skill set is not just there yet. Either way, it gives you your next goal, each time reaching that next level of improvement. Here is where desire is born. The perfect combination of skill, confidence, and just a touch of ignorance on fire that will get you there. Think Elon Musk, not Barney Fife. That will be a personal growth stimulator. You cannot build desire without positive feedback.

Ask yourself these questions every day: *What do I want? When do I want it? How will I get it? Who can help me get there?* Then, ask yourself, *What do I want more of and what do I need less of in my life?*

I'll leave you with this: we can get easily distracted. I talk about the lack of a personal excellence alarm clock that rings for you when it's time to get to work. Many of us are used to a yearly employee review for raises and measurement, but desire is killed with that "just enough to get by" mentality. We are the CEO and the top salesperson for our own lives. We need to hold ourselves accountable, and when you learn to have desire, that is all on autopilot. For those of you devotees to the book that this series is based upon, I give you this reference, and if it is too obscure, then read it again. Barnes had no "Plan B"—that is where his desire was born: all or nothing!

PAUL CAPOZIO

About Paul Capozio: Paul Capozio was born in Hoboken, New Jersey and grew up on the streets of Hudson County. At 35, he was recruited to be the President of Sales and Marketing for a 350-million-dollar human resources firm. In 7 years, he drove the top line revenue of that firm to over 1.5 billion.

Capozio owns and operates Capco Capital, Inc., an investment and consulting firm. The majority of Capco's holdings are of manufacturers and distributors of health and wellness products and human resources firms. Capco provides sales consulting and training, helping companies increase sales through traditional and direct sales disciplines. Making the invisible visible and simplifying the complex is his stock and trade.

A dynamic public speaker, he provides motivation and "meat and potatoes" skills to those in the health and wellness field who do not consider themselves "salespeople," allowing their voices to be heard above the "noise."

He is a husband of 32 years to his wife, Linda. He is also a father and grandfather.

Author's website: *www.PaulCapozio.com*
Book Series Website & Author's Bio: *www.The13StepsToRiches.com*

Robyn Scott

IT ALL COMES DOWN TO A FEELING

What do you dream of? What do you want? What are you wishing for? What is YOUR desire? Surprisingly, in this day and age, I have met many people who do not even know!

On the emotion vibrational scale, desire is a low, 125 out of 1000. (google: Emotion vibrational scale) It is right after fear. Think of a typical three- to four-year-old. They are so excited about everything around them! They marvel at a ladybug and jump for joy for bubbles being blown! They are curious and always asking, "Why, why, why?" They are discovering how the world works. By the time we are five years old, fear has crept into us from experiences, beliefs placed upon us, and programming that our immature minds try to interpret with an extremely skewed perspective. Unfortunately, we truly take all of these beliefs as "ours." Some may stay true for us. We have the ability to go through those beliefs to see if it is still true for us NOW!

Mr. Sherwood was my first-grade teacher. He was a large, burly, bearded teddy bear, and I loved him. I remember we were coloring a big banner for "back to school night." He came over to me, got down to my level, and said, "When we color in one direction, it looks a lot better." He demonstrated what he meant and got up and continued to walk around the group of us coloring. That is all it took. I was not good at art! I believed that for a very, VERY long time. Through the journey of self-awareness and personal development, I went to that moment and truly looked at it from all perspectives. I saw myself coloring with my classmates. I saw Mr. Sherwood. I watched as he knelt down beside me and heard the words.

I had created a belief that was not a truth for me in the slightest! My childish mind at five years old did not know how to file that interaction. I *now* could look at the situation and look upon my amazing teacher and know without a doubt he was teaching me. Nothing more! He had no ill will in his mind at all. He was taking care of me, and I loved him more for doing so. *And* I can tell you that I am pretty gosh darn good at art! It has been extremely satisfying to look at these kinds of moments and get to decide if the old belief is wholeheartedly a true belief for me *now*.

"I believe it is fear that stops us from desiring anything too big!" My dearest friend and genius mentor quotes Tanya Nelson, "The biggest key in my opinion to desire is we avoid it because of the deep longing and LACK we feel. Desire is a belief, not a feeling of lack, and it's the one place we can match the deep energy of abundance and receiving all that's ALREADY there and available to us. It is the birthplace for CREATION and RECEIVING."

When did it become taboo to desire extravagantly? I mean truly desire something awesome and big? Is it because of the stigma of being selfish? Guess what? Everything alive is selfish! We are all selfish! We only really know what it is that we want and when we need something.

I have five kids who are still alive (*oh man*, there were moments I thought about strangling each and every one of them, twice!), thriving, and I was and am still selfish. I washed clothes, scrubbed toilets, and vacuumed acres and acres of carpet. I cooked and got groceries, and I made sure they ate at mealtime. You could say I was doing it *for* them; however, honestly, I was doing it for *me*. I wanted my kids to have clean clothes. I wanted my children to eat. I wanted my family to play on a clean floor. I *wanted* to use a clean toilet! It benefited everyone, of course, and I was still selfish.

I am so very happy I did not strangle them, because now, I am going to be a grandma! That is extremely beneficial for me and SELFISH! It is very apparent in the animal kingdom; "*ABSOTIVELY*" it is true in the depths of the ocean and "*POSITUTELY*" how it works for all amphibians and reptiles! When we understand that, that is the truth, it allows us to completely feel "*SPECTABULOUSLY*" okay to have a burning desire for whatever we want!

"Weak desires bring weak results, just as a weak fire brings a small amount of heat." -Napoleon Hill

Desire is the belief that we can create literally anything we want!! I ask you to answer these questions for YOU!!! You have my permission to write it down! Right here! Right NOW!

What do you dream of?

What do you want?

What are you wishing for?

What is YOUR burning desire?

As you explore your desires, put away logic for just a moment. I challenge you to dream wildly! Desire *HUMONGOUSLY!* Read chapter two again in *Think and Grow Rich*. If you get stumped (you are not alone by a long shot), bring close, connected people of yours into the process. If you have access to kids, they are *perfect* to ask! Start simple, and with each answer, ask yourself, "What could be better than that?" at least three times. Five is even more effective! Have fun! I can't wait for you to discover your authentic, deep desire!

Want to go deeper? Of course, you do! Read your desire you just found and ask the question "Why?" Can you see your answer? Ask again. "Why do I desire this?" And then ask again. Five levels of "Why do I desire this?" I will give you a hint... ready... here it is... it all comes down to a feeling!

ROBYN SCOTT

About Robyn Scott: Robyn is the Chief Relationship Officer for Champion Circle. She manages the prospecting program for Divinely Driven Results. Scott is a Habit Finder Coach and has worked closely with the president, Paul Blanchard, at the Og Mandino Group. She is also a certified Master Your Emotions Coach, through Inscape World. Scott is commonly known in professional communities as the Queen of Connection and Princess of Play. She has been working hard for the past 9 years to hone her skills as a mentor and coach.

Scott strives to teach people to annihilate judgements, embrace their own stories, and empower themselves to rediscover who they truly are. Scott is an international speaker and also teaches how to present yourself on stage.

Her first book, *Bringing People Together: Rediscovering the Lost Art of Face-to-Face Connecting, Collaborating, and Creating* was released in August of 2019 and was a bestseller in seven categories.

Author's website: *www.MyChampionCircle.com/Robyn-Scott*
Book Series Website & Author's Bio: *www.The13StepsToRiches.com*

THE SCENT OF DESIRE

Desire, to quote Napoleon Hill, is "the starting point of all achievement." Desire is like a spark of fire that can bring light to an entire city; the will to achieve is deeply and securely rooted in our DNA. In everything we accomplish, from the monumental (founding our own company) to the mundane (deciding what to have for breakfast), desire is the foundation of it all.

The concept of desire sometimes gets a bad rap, though. Sure, too much desire—like too much of anything—can often lead us down a bad and un-valuable path, but when coupled with a sense of healthy curiosity, humility, and the willingness to grow and adapt, desire can be the first step in achieving anything we want.

It's important to understand that there is a big difference between desire and desperation, though. When I was younger, I decided that I wanted to be a model. I moved to New York, got an agent, took some professional pictures, and I was off to the races. Audition after audition after audition. But for the life of me, I simply couldn't land a gig, no matter how hard I tried. What was I doing wrong? Not working hard enough? Not passionate or energetic enough?

No matter how hard I tried, I just couldn't get booked. Frustrated and depressed, I tried even harder. I dialed my energy up to eleven. I showed up early to every single audition, and I tried even harder to win the clients over, hoping beyond hope that might work in my favor. And yet, try as I might, year after year, I would get rejected over and over again. In fact, my booker said to me one day, "Shannon, what do you do when you go to the audition? The clients love your look, but you blow it when they meet you in person." I stood there perplexed. I didn't have the answer. I had no idea.

One of my buddies witnessed my struggles. I told her how hard I was trying, and how much I tried to persuade the client to choose me.

"I don't get it," I said. "Why can't I get booked?"

After listening to everything I had to say, she looked me in the eye and told me point blank that I "reeked" of desperation, that desperation is a "perfume," and that people can smell it a mile away. "Until you wash that perfume off of you," she continued, "you're not going to land a single job."

I was taken aback. Desperate? Me? I saw myself as motivated, sure, but certainly not desperate. And even if I was being a little desperate, isn't that a good thing? Don't clients want to see how much I want the job and how much I'm willing to prove my worthiness?

The truth, however, is that desperation is equal to idolatry. Regardless of our own personal religious or spiritual affiliations or practices, some of us are guilty, at times, of creating "idols" of things we desire: a new house, more social media followers, a fun dating life, or in my case, a successful modeling career. There is nothing wrong with wanting these things, but when we go from desire to desperation, we take healthy wants and turn them into twenty-first century golden calves.

Losing sight of the bigger picture, we obsessively place things that are limited, finite, and perishable on pedestals, because they'll supposedly make us happier or more successful. In doing so, we convince ourselves—even implicitly—that we are worthless without them. We fall into a dangerous trap of internalization, castigating ourselves for failing to achieve our goals. In the process, we lower ourselves and internalize when we are unable to achieve them.

We don't have to fall into this trap. Instead of letting desire control us, we have the capacity to control it, and in doing so, make us more empowered to fulfill our dreams. We can more easily see the big picture, set realistic yet ambitious goals, and bring about what we most deeply desire. Like most things in life, there is no cure-all for honing desire; different methods work for different people. I have a few quick tips that have helped me achieve my goals, and if you find yourself stuck wearing the scent of desperation like I was, these tips may just help you out.

Determine Your "Why"

We all desire things for a reason—sometimes, that reason is healthy, and sometimes, it's not. Let's say there's someone in your life you're very attracted to and you want nothing more in the world than to be in a long-term relationship with them. Maybe you built up the nerve to ask this person out, only for them to dodge the question or reject you, leaving you feeling empty, insecure, and perhaps seeing yourself as unworthy of even asking them out in the first place.

In cases like this, it's helpful to determine the root of the issue by asking yourself a series of "why" questions. Why do you feel the way you do? Why do you like this person in the first place? Why do you think being with them would make you happy? And ultimately: Why do you want to be in a relationship?

Many of us do not want to be alone, but sometimes, without even realizing it, we may have turned the concept of being in a romantic relationship into a golden calf and convinced ourselves we are nothing without it. The good news is that once we realize we had a toxic "why," we can more easily see that our self-worth is not dependent on whether or not we achieve our goal. We can re-approach the concept of dating as something fun, exciting, and full of possibilities, and no longer the obsession that was bringing us down.

Meditation

Another thing that has helped me with desire is meditation. Imagining and visualizing everything I want. And feeling and acting as if it has already happened. Not to sound too woo woo, because I know meditation can be challenging for some. And if you're one of the many people with some form of ADD or ADHD, the act of sitting, focusing, and silencing unwanted thoughts can be especially difficult. But like all things, practice makes permanent, and honing this restorative and empowering skill will help you more easily and organically manifest your desires.

When I meditate, I often like to focus on the idea of oneness. I close my eyes, unclench my jaw, either sit with my palms open or lay on my back (I try not to fall asleep!), and I focus on the concept that everything in the Universe is interconnected—that the very same energy that created the Universe is the very same energy working through us every moment of every day. Therefore, we are already connected to the thing(s) we most desire! All we have to do is focus on why we want to achieve it, what it would mean, and how it would feel to have it, and affirm that we are more than capable of taking the journey to achieve it.

That's how I attracted my wife. I made a list of all of the characteristics I wanted. I meditated on the list every single day and I told people I was getting married. I hadn't even met her yet! But low and behold, one day, just like that: *poof*, she appeared. Twenty-two years later and life is beautiful!

Love and Honor Yourself

The reason some of us have yet to achieve our desires stems from the idea that we're not worthy enough to have them in the first place. Ever felt like that? Perhaps you grew up in an emotionally unhealthy home where you had to be the caretaker for your family, putting your needs and wants aside in the process. Perhaps you were bullied, like me, or unpopular in school and now have a stunted sense of self-worth because of deep-seated childhood wounds. Whatever the reason, sometimes, our trauma will convince us that we don't deserve the things we most desire; that we're not smart, strong, or competent enough to achieve them.

The thing to remember, however, is that we are not our trauma. It's something that happened to us, not by us, and has no bearing on who we are or what we desire. By owning this fact, by beginning the hard yet rewarding work of releasing ourselves from this blame, we put ourselves in a much better position to give ourselves the love and honor we deserve and not depend on it from those who never gave it to us in the first place.

A few ways I show myself love is by reflecting on what I've already achieved, despite the obstacles put in my way. Despite every time someone told me no, despite every moment I was backstabbed, ridiculed, or ignored by my peers, despite every night I cried myself to sleep because of the harmful words and actions of others, I achieved things I would have never imagined in a billion years. And if I was able to overcome all of that while failing to love myself, imagine what I can accomplish when I do love me!

No matter what you desire, you are capable of achieving it— not through desperation, but through natural manifestation. By understanding the root of your desire, by cultivating nourishing practices of self-care, and by loving yourself despite every alleged reason not to, you inch yourself ever closer to making your desire a reality. How beautiful is that?

SHANNON WHITTINGTON

About Shannon Whittington: Shannon (she/her) is a speaker, author, consultant, and clinical nurse educator. Her area of expertise is LGBTQ+ inclusion in the workplace. Whittington has a passion for transgender health where she educates clinicians in how to care for transgender individuals after undergoing gender-affirming surgeries.

Whittington was honored to receive the Quality and Innovation Award from the Home Care Association of New York for her work with the transgender population. She was recently awarded the Notable LGBTQ+ Leaders & Executives award by Crain's New York Business, as well as the International Association of Professionals Nurse of the Year award. Whittington is a city and state lobbyist for transgender equality.

To date, Whittington has presented virtually and in person at various organizations and conferences across the nation, delivering extremely well-received presentations. Her forthcoming books include *LGBTQ+: ABC's For Grownups* and *Kindergarten for Leaders: 9 Essential Tips For Grownup Success.*

Author's Website: *www.linkedin.com/in/shannonwhittington*
Book Series Website & Author's Bio: *www.The13StepsToRiches.com*

Soraiya Vasanji

THE JOURNEY OF SELF-LOVE IS DOUBLE THE WORTH

Like most little girls playing pretend house, I knew early on that I wanted to be a mom one day. It was a desire in the deepest part of my heart that I would dream about now and then but would return it to the furthest shelf in my mind, like a borrowed book. I started to reflect on where this desire came from and how desires shape our satisfaction in life. But what is desire?

When I think about my desires, I think about what I truly, deeply want to have and create in this world. At first, this feels quite selfish: I desire to be loved, to find my soulmate, to live a purposeful life, to be a mother—it's all about me. The more I reflect on my desire, I discover the vision at the core of my being. I desire to show anyone and everyone I meet that they are worthy of receiving love, just like me. This is the deepest part of my desire, and the source of my power. Everything stems from this place. When I am aligned with this belief about who I am and what I am meant to do in this world, every act is full of love. I am the love that I see missing around me.

What I now realize is that this desire was born out of me wanting to be seen, wanting to be heard, and wanting to know without a doubt that I am fit to be loved. Therefore, I invite you to uncover the root of your desires. Desire connects to our vision, and it is imperative that it is clear.

It is necessary to have clarity on our life's vision and desires and refine this vision, so it is aligned with our thoughts and actions. When there is a mismatch between what we expect and what we do, we create negative emotions like resentment and self-doubt. For example, if our vision is to be loved, getting clarity on what that looks like, includes questions like: *How do I perceive love? What does being loved look like? And if I'm not feeling loved, what story do I make up about myself?* Understanding the construct of our desire enables us to identify if we are on track or need to course correct. Our vision acts as the compass to achieve our desire. Without a clear vision for our desire, it is challenging to bring to fruition.

Looking back, it is so clear that I had a deep desire to be loved, and that I equated being smart with being loved. I set about proving how smart I was to myself and others by earning high grades, joining clubs like Model United Nations, where my intellect was valued, and setting my sights on joining the National Honor Society (NHS). Every year, I analyzed what grades it would take to get there and found solutions for all the challenges that came up. I remember the day I found out I had earned entry into the NHS and I was beaming with pride and excitement. I shared it with my family, and I felt pride in my intellectual achievements. At this time in my life, I was seeking self-worth through knowing that I had the smarts to make it in a competitive world.

Throughout my childhood, I often heard academic success being the only path forward to professional success. It was the tenets of self-discipline, relentless faith, and being laser-focused on the goal that continually supported me to achieve. Yet, my desire to feel worthy remained unfulfilled. This pattern continued from my student life to my professional life.

As the youngest pharmaceutical specialty sales representative in the renal therapeutic business, the desire to prove myself and show my intellect was evident. I consistently sought external validation for each goal that was set in front of me. Achieving the goal wasn't enough; I had to knock it out of the park.

This desire to achieve a high level of success in my career pops up numerous times, and while this external validation provides temporary satisfaction, what I have come to learn is that the true indicator of achievement is accepting myself and celebrating all my accomplishments. Furthermore, I realize that failing to be present and celebrate my achievements prevented me from experiencing the self-love that I was seeking. I lovingly share that finding pleasure and peace within is what shall liberate your self-worth.

What I have come to learn through the years is that desire can be both active and passive. Unlike my academic achievements that were desires I actively pursued, my journey in finding my soulmate came naturally and unexpectedly. When you are so clear about what you are looking for, it is like the Universe conspires to support you and sends you big flashing messages. My husband, Nadim, laughs at this, but I tell him I just knew when I met him freshman year that he was the one. It felt like a moment in a movie scene where it's just the two of us sitting at a bench in Harvard

Square drinking Burdick's hot chocolate. With the hustle and bustle surrounding us, yet all we can hear is the stories we share.

We married a year out of college and wanting a family was something I would think about and yet the competing desire to achieve certain things in life before having children was calling me forward, louder than any other voice. In my mid-twenties, I felt like I had all the time in the world to welcome my dimpled, long-lashed little ones. What I didn't know then is that the journey to motherhood would be a saga fraught with chapters of pain, and that this is where the prelude of my true purpose in this world was born.

Becoming a mom was written in my DNA. What I wanted more than anything was to share my love with my children. We were blessed with our first pregnancy after a difficult fertility process. I became pregnant with our twins, Nadiya and Raina, and was ecstatic. I remember having their twentieth weekly ultrasound with the Stanford neonatologists, and everything was on target. I was confident and feeling blessed at how the pregnancy was going. What I didn't appreciate was that things can change in an instant.

Shortly after this ultrasound, I went into premature labor. I experienced the body-contorting contractions, the see-saw pattern of pushing and breathing, and finally, birthing my twins. Their lungs were not capable of breathing on their own, and as parents, we held them and prayed for their souls, but, ultimately, we had to let them go. This was my first decision as a mother, and it was to let my babies go. I continued to have faith and trusted that my desire to be a mom would happen one day. Never give up and know that if something is to be, you get to hold firmly to that desire.

The loss of the twins awakened my calling to discover my strength as a life coach and, ultimately, find healing through self-compassion and self-love. Surprisingly, after all of the tragedy and heartache it took to become a mother, I found myself getting frustrated, overwhelmed, impatient, lacking time and energy, and beating myself up for not being "the perfect mother" to my darling miracle baby. By experiencing this, and the dark days of grief, I've made it my mission to inspire women to know they, we, are worthy of unconditional love. What I have discovered on my path to becoming a mother and life coach is that the ability to serve and give to others is only sustainable if we love ourselves first.

Now, as an adult, I can see that the desire for love manifests itself in various forms and sometimes, love is found not only through joyous celebratory achievements, but in the darkest moments of grief. When we surrender to the desire and let go of expectations, we experience an abundance of joy. There is no more time to waste or wait for the perfect moment. The joy is in the now.

Something I would invite my younger self to explore is to be unattached to the outcome. To come from a place where I can be fully unattached to how I think something should look, sound, or be like. Why? Because once you have clarity on what your desire is, there is an immense freedom and joy in letting go of how that desire manifests. In trusting and being open to how it gets to bloom. Deeply knowing and investing in our desire is important, but it would save a lot of agony, frustration, and confusion if we focused on the feelings we receive, instead of the goal itself.

SORAIYA VASANJI

About Soraiya Vasanji: Soraiya is a Certified Professional Coach (CPC), Energy Leadership Index Master Practitioner (ELI-MP), and has a Master's in Business Administration (MBA) from Kellogg University. She inspires women to be present, not perfect, ditch what doesn't serve them, and create their best messy life now. She loves sharing her wisdom on mindset, the power of language, self-love, self-worth, and leadership principles. She is the founder of the Mommy Mindset Summit series, where she interviews experts on topics that interest moms, so they can create a life of authenticity, abundance, and joy—and show their kids how to have it all, too.

Soraiya is married to her soulmate, has a four-year-old daughter, and lives in Toronto, Canada. She is a foodie and a jetsetter, and she loves collecting unique crafting and stationery products!

Author's Website: *www.SoraiyaVasanji.com*
Book Series Website & Author's Bio: *www.The13StepsToRiches.com*

Teresa Cundiff

DESIRE IS WHERE YOU MAKE IT

Let's be honest here, shall we? The word DESIRE connotates itself with the word sex! It just does! So there, I've said it and gotten it out of the way, so now we can move on and talk about what we are here to talk about regarding desire.

I want you to think about what it is that you have a burning desire for right now in your life! RIGHT NOW! It's okay… stop… look up… look around the room… lean back in your chair… search your mind…search your heart. Or maybe your burning desire came to you immediately. *Boom!* Just like that! You want to make a million dollars, and nothing is going to stop you! Or you want to have the latest model iPhone the second it's available! Or maybe, you must have a brand-new car every year!

There is no one-size-fits-all for your burning desire. AND, one's burning desire of five, ten, or twenty years ago may not be one's burning desire of today. Let's take me for example… that makes the most sense, since I'm the one writing this chapter, and I'm the number one authority on me!

My current burning desire as of this writing in May 2021 is my digital TV show *Teresa Talks*. It consumes my every waking moment. I have lists of tasks; I am thinking about how I want to conduct my interviews; I am thinking about all the amazing people I want to bring onto my show and hope that when I approach them, they will say "yes," and it goes on and on. Was this a burning desire last year you ask? No siree-bob! It wasn't even a blip on my radar.

Two years ago, I started a new job. It was my burning desire at that time to, (a) get hired and (b) perform all tasks to the best of my ability and (c) be the best person they had ever hired. Super-duper overachiever right here. I was going to get trained up faster than anyone ever had and WOW everyone around me.

Thirty-two years ago, my burning desire was to marry one man from whom I would never get divorced. Whooooaaaaaa, you say. How can a person do that? No one can predict the future. And that is 100 percent true, but you see, I am a Christian woman, and I claim the verse in Psalm 37:4 that says, "Delight yourself in the Lord, and He will give you the desires of your heart."

It was my heart's desire to only be married one time, and I was willing to wait for that one man. I knew God knew who that one man was, and that was good enough for me. I had had my opportunity to marry the wrong man a couple of times, and it's very intoxicating to sing at all your sorority sister's weddings and want to be a bride sooner rather than later, but I knew in my heart of hearts that those men weren't who God had for me.

It's how I have lived my life when it comes to burning desire. Things begin to come together, and the Universe conspires FOR me, but

I know that as a believer, that it's God working His will in my life. The doors begin to open, and amazing things begin to happen. My mind and heart begin to fixate and align on the burning desire that has been placed in my heart.

I will admit that I am a "maneuver-er." That's a word I just made up to explain how when I get my mind set on something that I think I've got to have, that I start "maneuvering" things to try and get what I want, but oftentimes, that's forcing that square peg into that round hole, and it doesn't work. Are you with me? Do you do that, too? I will just keep banging my head up against that wall, because I think I must have a thing, but that has turned out to be a "fake burning desire," and I have to let it go. It's like the Garth Brooks song, "Thank God for Unanswered Prayers."

The TV show snuck up on me from way out of the clear blue. That's how I know it was a God thing. My side gig is as a freelance proofreader. A lot of my friends had been going on social media saying that they were starting up TV shows, which in my younger days, would have made me so green with envy and even jealousy and wanting to figure out how to get my own TV show. But I hadn't felt that desire welling up inside me.

One day, I hopped on Messenger to congratulate my precious friend, and she picked up the phone and called me. Long story short, by the end of the day, I, too, had a TV show. It began to create in me a burning desire that I didn't know I had. And God is turning it into something amazing, and I'm working with people who uplift me and support me, but most importantly, who truly love me.

So, there you are reading this and thinking, well la-de-da, good for you, Teresa. And for that, I say, thank you. But here's what's in it for you…you could have a new burning desire placed in your heart and mind tomorrow that you don't even see coming. Or, right now, you could have the seed of a burning desire rolling around in your mind, waiting for you to take hold of it and give it some nurturing thoughts or to talk over with a mentor.

Which brings me to a place to give credit where credit is due. There is no way in this whole wide world I would be where I am without the amazing Forbes Riley. She was my first mentor when I didn't even know what having a mentor on such a grand scale was like. She swooped in and transformed my thinking and introduced me to people who helped me begin to transform my life. If you are reading this and you do not have a mentor, reach out to me. I will point you in the right direction.

Take a moment and take stock of your life up to now. Can you see how your desires have changed in your own life? I can think back to before I was pregnant and wanting our first child to be a boy, but then, once I became pregnant, I just wanted to be blessed with a healthy baby. I wanted a career and a big house. But then I fell in love with an Army officer and home was wherever he was, and the structure we lived in made no difference. The boys came along, and raising them became of paramount importance to me, not going to an office. I didn't have the life I thought I desired when I was in college and grad school; I had so much more.

When we start out, we see our lives through a lens of possibility and desire, right? And even some preconceived notions of what we do with our college degrees and "what's expected of us." But as we mature and we grow and we refocus our lens, we see more clearly how our understanding of life and our contribution to it has become more valuable, because we know our hearts and minds. I tell people, "No" when I know things are not a good fit for me. I do a gut check to see if the request is going to thwart my burning desire or to see if it will ignite a new burning desire. Both are necessary.

All the authors in this book are going to speak about desire in different ways, but what I want you to take from me is that your desires are just that: yours. They can be as grandiose or as simple as you decide they are. Don't feel guilty if your burning desire is wealth. One of my burning desires is wealth. I prayerfully hope that I am on the path to wealth. But regardless, I am meeting so many incredible people along the way that the journey is absolutely priceless. So much good has been done in the world by people of wealth. Actually, don't feel guilty, regardless of what you desire. Do everything in your power to fulfill all your desires. Work diligently every day toward what brings you joy. And trust me when I say, "I'm preaching to the choir."

Running a close second on my burning desire list is to quit my day job, which will land me right smack dab in the middle of doing what I love. And that is the plan. So, let me be an encouragement to you, keep the faith (which we will discuss in the next book, and I have lots to say about that!), and never lose sight of what you desire most. You will have many types of desires. Treasure them all. Give them their proper respect and place that they deserve in your heart and mind.

TERESA CUNDIFF

About Teresa Cundiff: Teresa hosts an interview digital TV show called Teresa Talks on Legrity TV. On the show, she interviews authors who are published and unpublished—and that just means those authors haven't put their books on paper yet. The show provides a platform for authors to have a global reach with their message. Teresa Talks is produced by Wordy Nerds Media Inc., of which Cundiff is the CEO.

Cundiff is also a freelance proofreader with the tagline, "I know where the commas go!," Teresa makes her clients' work shine with her knowledge of grammar, punctuation, and sentence structure.

Teresa is a two-time International Best-Selling Contributing Author of 1 Habit for Entrepreneurial Success and 1 Habit to Thrive in a Post-COVID World. She is also a best-selling contributing author of The Art of Connection; 365 Days of Networking Quotes, which has been placed in the Library of Congress.

Author's Website: *www.TeresaTalksTV.com*
Book Series Website & Author's Bio: *www.The13StepsToRiches.com*

Vera Thomas

HOLD FAST TO YOUR DREAMS

Hold fast to your dreams.
Even if at times, it seems they may never come true.
Living your dreams will depend on you.
The roads that we take, the paths that we choose,
Are necessary to live our dreams through.
There may be detours, winding roads, and wrong turns.
All on which lessons are to be learned.
As your journey unfolds,
You will realize your goals.
What a beautiful story soon to be told!
Hold fast!
Hold fast!
To your dreams!

For dreams to become a reality
You got to take action
things will happen.
Persist, and you will gain.
Pursue your goals day by day,
Your life will not be the same!
Dream dreams without hesitation.

Visualize them!
See them EVERY DAY!
FEEEEEEL
the excitement
Exaltation,
While you are on Your Way.

Vera Thomas
© 1990

Once I recognized my purpose, I recognized my dreams and my desire to make a difference!

Desire, burning desire in the midst of detours, winding roads, wrong turns, and lessons learned. I want to talk about those things that can defer a dream, not the desire. This is a portion of my story.

Growing up with no confidence, self-esteem, or recognition of my self-worth, I could not imagine a life with a burning desire to make a difference. I was bullied and ridiculed by other children and adults. I remember asking God, "Why was I born? What is my purpose?"

It was not until I read the book *The Magic of Believing*, by Claude Bristol, that I began to recognize a desire within. It was the beginning of my journey into self-development. The book *Think and Grow Rich* had a lasting impact to the point of me memorizing the poem "Think" that is in the book.

However, I still did not know my purpose or reason for living. I worked a couple of years out of high school before going to college.

I started college at Kent State University, Stark County Branch, and became the first Black president of student government.

I had the opportunity to go to Los Angeles, and I dropped out of college. I was there for seven months still not knowing my purpose. Seven months later, I had to return home, as my mother's cancer had returned. She died seven months later at the age of forty-three.

Going to Los Angeles was a life-changing experience. I grew up in a predominantly White community where African-Americans had limited opportunities. In Los Angeles, I saw people who looked like me in a myriad of community and leadership roles. I met Jesse Jackson and Maxine Waters; the Honorable Tom Bradley was the mayor. While I still did not know my purpose, I did have a desire to be involved in the community and to make a difference.

After returning home, I got a summer job organizing events for children at a local park. As a result of my work, people were looking for me to offer me a job. Seven opportunities came my way. The position I took was with the county board of education as a project manager for a special project. It was there that I attended a work required three-day training called "Adventures in Attitude," with a facilitator that was so enthusiastic and bubbly that a fire was set in my belly.

After the training, I approached the facilitator and said, "I want to do what you do!" She became my mentor. As my mentor, Becky (RIH) steered me in the direction of perfecting my speaking and presentation skills, including introducing me to Toastmasters and a two-year program designed to prepare one to become a member of NSA (National Speakers Association). While I did not have the money to become a member of NSA, I knew I was well on my way.

I began my training and speaking career by becoming certified in pre-packaged training programs, including Performax "Adventures in Attitudes," Zig Ziglar's "See You at the Top," and Mary Kay Slowikowski's "Future Woman."

My very first session was with a group of underprivileged youth. I remember the Saturday about a week after doing the training with the children; I was walking around in my apartment still asking, *What is my purpose?* On that day, in the mail, were several letters from the children, expressing how they felt about the training. I cried. That is when I knew my purpose and my desire.

I facilitated "Zig Ziglar's "See You at the Top" as a continuing education class at one of the local universities. I was twenty-five. The youngest participant was in their forties and the oldest in her seventies. I looked much younger than my age. On the first day of class, I could read their faces. *What is this young Black girl going to do for us?* I immediately acknowledged their trepidation. There was a life-changing transformation. Again, confirmation I was living out my purpose.

I continued facilitating training programs and received a major contract to provide ten-day sessions for people who were seeking employment and/or training. Things were going great. My desire to make a difference was in full bloom—or so I thought.

Wrong Turn: I met someone and got married. Two weeks after the wedding, he told me he did not want to work and wanted to focus on his music! He was also verbally, emotionally, and mentally abusive. While my desire was still there, with the weight of the relationship, I was no longer authentic in my ability to continue my journey of speaking and training. He had an opportunity in Los Angeles, and we moved there from Ohio.

The deal fell through, and he went into a state of depression. I worked to support us. My desire to continue to work in the field of training and speaking never left me. I became pregnant; he became more abusive.

He attacked me in front of my son when my son was three months old. At that point, I knew I did not want to raise a child in that kind of environment. I became a single parent when my son was six months old.

That marriage was a wrong turn that I allowed to stifle my desire. I lost my confidence and self-esteem and had to start all over on my self-development journey. This time, not only for myself; more importantly, for my son.

Lesson learned: Listen to that still small voice inside. The day I got married, I heard, *You should not be doing this!* There I was, with a church full of people, birds chirping with the music we created for our wedding, ten bridesmaids, and I am hearing I should not be doing this! Well, the best thing that happened out of that marriage was my son, who I raised as a single mother. He is one of the most positive people I know.

After separating from my husband, he left the state. I stayed in Los Angeles for another couple of years. My desire never left; however, living in Los Angeles as a single mother was quite a challenge. Things were not good. I created a vision board and put everything I thought I wanted on the board. I then listened to the still, small voice that told me to leave Los Angeles.

Winding Road: Once I returned to Ohio, things took a turn for the better, including getting back to my love and desire for speaking and training. As a Career Development Training Specialist, I was living my desire to train, speak, and make a difference in the lives of others. The winding road included community involvement, taking ten years to finally get my degree, and another five for my Master's.

I created my flagship program for children called "Poetry and my Vision," which I facilitated in schools for over eight years. I became involved in the fatherhood initiative that culminated in over 10,000 fathers participating in "The Father's Walk."

Lesson learned: As a result of working with children and fathers, I am acutely aware of the need to address the issue of parents and their children. I have since developed a program called "Instilling Greatness in Myself and My Children."

I continued to work with companies, organizations, schools, and churches speaking and training.

Detour: In 2011, both my sisters—younger than me—were diagnosed with cancer. One lived in Ohio, the other in Kentucky. I found myself traveling back and forth as they went through their ordeal. I moved to Kentucky to be closer to my youngest sister. I basically put my desire and dreams on hold for seven years to care for them. They both lost their battles.

Lesson learned: Life has its twists and turns, and tomorrow is not promised. Everything we go through by choice or destiny is to get us closer to our desires and to instill in us what we strive to instill in others. I thank God that time has given me the opportunity to pursue my desire, and now is my time to do just that!

VERA THOMAS

About Vera Thomas: As a Life Coach, Speaker, Trainer, Mediator, Poet, and Producer of a weekly podcast/radio show called "The Vera Thomas Show," Vera has worked with companies, non-profit organizations, schools, and churches customizing and delivering training and leadership programs.

Enduring physical, emotional, and mental abuse as a child, rape, homelessness and surviving as a battered wife leaving her husband when her son was only 6 months old, Vera has organized a program called the "Father's Walk!" This program would focus on fathers walking their child to school on a specific date. Impacting over 10,000 fathers who took part in the program, it allowed the movement to change systemic attitudes and behaviors towards fathers in family court, child support, and children services.

Author's Website: *www.VeraThomasCoaching.com*
Book Series Website & Author's Bio: *www.The13StepstoRiches.com*

DESIRE IS THE FORCE OF EXPANSION

You are hungry for it. You want it. You wake up thinking about it. You can hardly sleep because you are excited about it. You are craving it. Everything in your body aches for it. There is that deep life force energy moving profoundly inside of you, which feels like a burning fire that is ready to start a wildfire all around you. You can feel the intense heat in your belly and in your heart. Your body moves with passion, and the energy of your soul pours through all your movements. These movements activate such power and action within you and those around you can feel it. This burning desire, this fire within you, is what moves you into action towards your vision. This desire is what activates you to create, build, architect, and grow in this Universe.

This is how I'd describe a burning desire that leads to action. Many want to create this feeling from within, and they want to feel this intense zest and vitality in life. Yet, oftentimes, many lose this passion and drive. And why? Sometimes, it is the years or decades of mundane, routine-like life that blows out the spark over time. I've seen people go to work without any passion. They go through their daily lives without any reflection or intention, and they repeat this cycle without questioning it.

Although what got those people there originally was their own initial desire to be there, over time, they don't nurture and continue to ignite their desire into something bigger. Or their desire gets dimmed and loses its energy due to the fear of what's happened in the past. These people start their days with, *Ugh, here we go again with another day.*

They get ready, dragging their feet to the shower. They dread going to work. They have lost that fire, and they feel stuck in a wash-rinse-repeat cycle. That burning desire is now nowhere to be found. And then they wonder, *Why is life so difficult and not fun? Why is life so hard to get through?* How do I know all this? Because I used to be one of them, and these are the stories of my clients.

You see, desire is the single most activating force behind all creations, expansion, and manifestations in this Universe. Take a moment to pause and look at the reality around you. Everything and anything around you started with what was once a thought, that turned into a burning desire, that got activated into creation.

For example, take a look at your iPhone. It was once Steve Jobs' *idea*, then, his idea caught on fire that turned into *desire* when his passion for innovation took over, and it launched it into creation.

Look at the book that you're reading. It was once just a *thought*, and when it was infused with the excitement of what it could be, it turned into a *desire*. And the truth is, people have brilliant thoughts and ideas *all the time*. In fact, while we have anywhere between 60,000 to 80,000 thoughts a day, though not all of those transform into desires and manifest into new creations.

Those people stuck in their mundane lives that I described above may have had many *thoughts* of doing something else, or doing things differently, other than continuing to live the life they once created that keeps them feeling stuck. Yet, what keeps them out of living a full life exploring his or her full potential, and constantly expanding in different ways? They never nurtured their thoughts enough to let them become *desires*.

So, the question is: how do we turn these thoughts into burning desires, so that they lead us to massive action and a life that we get to deeply love?

Thoughts turn into desires, when infused with strong life force energy, or an emotion. When these desires are further alchemized with intense focus, persistence, and attention, they turn into *burning* desires, as Napoleon Hill says, and they activate and cause new creations and expansion in this reality.

Everything and anything that has been created and architected in this reality started with a desire that was ignited, and that fire was persistently nurtured through focus and attention. Desire is, therefore, the single most crucial component of the motion towards this ever-expanding Universe. Desires are what expand the cutting edge of the Universe.

As a performance coach for entrepreneurs and high achievers, oftentimes, my clients initially come find me because they have lost this *spark*, this *edge*, and this *passion*. They start to dread their life, work, or business, or feel lost and stuck. They may start to feel anxiety or stress, because they have many *thoughts*, yet they don't fully potentiate them into *desires*.

What they don't know is that it is through reconnecting to the deepest desires of their souls, they can get fired up and get back on the path to becoming their best selves and achieve success.

When I finally quit my corporate job after a decade to start my coaching business and took the entrepreneurial path, it felt like I was finally freeing my deepest desires out into the world. I had desires to help people and be my own boss, yet I had been suppressing them for a long time. During this period of suppressing these desires, my days were clouded with mundanity and stress.

In that cathartic experience of finally honoring my desires that were waiting to be ignited, I found myself feeling so free and ecstatic as I quit and launched myself forward onto the next adventure in my life and business. Since then, I have been nurturing a beautiful relationship to my desires, so that they can be fully expressed.

And these voices of desires within us come from somewhere deep within our souls. When they are still faint, they remain as fleeting thoughts. When they get a bit louder, they become *desires*. When they get loud, wild, and unapologetic and start to have a spirit of their own, they become *burning desires* that help us discover the next most expansive versions of ourselves. So, when you feel stuck in any way, I invite you to call upon what desires that are deeply hidden within your soul that you've put away or suppressed.

Do you have a deep desire to make a positive impact in this world? Do you have a passion to help people transform in massive ways? Do you have a burning desire to take your business to the next level? Let these desires surface, and have a voice and take up space. It is in the reflection on our desires and taking the time to ignite them with passion that will propel us forward into success and happiness in business and life.

"Your Wish (Desire) is My Command."

These are the infamous words of the genie that grants wishes. If you had three wishes, what would you wish for? Did you know that it's been documented that in the original story of the genie, there were no limits to how many wishes could be granted? What if the Universe is constantly conspiring for all of our wishes and desires? What if we can have everything and anything that we want in this abundant Universe, as long as we have a strong enough and clear enough *desire* for it?

The Universe *wants* to help us manifest our desires. The clearer and stronger our desires are, the Universe reorganizes itself to help our desires come to life. So, when we lose our connection to our desires, we are not contributing to the most natural state of the Universe: expansion. So next time you start to get stuck and have a hard time re-connecting to your desires, I invite you to start asking yourself these two questions that I often pose to my clients to reignite their souls.

The first question is, **"What do I desire the most right now, at this moment?"** When I invite my clients to answer this question, they find themselves getting still for a second, and they get to check in with their heart and their soul to see what desires are being suppressed or hidden away that can be brought to life. As their desires surface, my clients feel as if they found the internal compass that guides them toward the next step or the next action to be taken.

The second question that I invite you to journal about is, "**What makes me feel most alive in this moment?**" This question beckons our souls to remember what our souls naturally crave the most. The answers may range from a quiet walk in nature, to traveling to a new city, to dancing, to connecting with a loved one.

Allow this question to help you remember what ignites your soul the most, and do just that, one by one, until you start to feel that spark and that fire within your body again. Do whatever that question leads you to, and enjoy the feeling of your soul getting turned on and coming alive in that moment. Notice that this feeling and energy initiates your being into connecting back to your desires. Your desires serve you to help you remember who you really are; you are the vessel for all the creative energy to be channeled through as desires, and in that you are the engine that causes action towards infinite expansion in this Universe.

YURI CHOI

About Yuri Choi: Yuri is the Founder of Yuri Choi Coaching. Yuri is a performance coach for entrepreneurs and high achievers. She helps them create and stay in a powerful, abundant, unstoppable mindset to achieve their goals by helping them gain clarity and understanding, leverage their emotional states, and create empowering habits and language patterns.

She is a speaker, writer, creator, connector, YouTuber, and the author of Creating Your Own Happiness. Yuri is passionate about spreading the messages about meditation, power of intention, and creating a powerful mindset to live a fulfilling life. She is also a Habitude Warrior Conference Speaker and emcee, and she is also a designated guest coach for Psych2Go, the largest online mental health magazine and YouTube Channel. Her mission in the world is to inspire people to live leading with L.O.V.E. (which stands for: laughter, oneness, vulnerability, and ease) and to ignite people's souls to live in a world of infinite creative possibilities and abundance.

Author's Website: *www.YuriChoiCoaching.com*
Book Series Website & Author's Bio: *www.The13StepsToRiches.com*

THE 13 STEPS TO RICHES
FEATURING:

DENIS WAITLEY ~ Author of *Psychology of Winning* & *The NEW Psychology of Winning - Top Qualities of a 21st Century Winner*, NASA's Performance Coach, Featured in *The Secret* ~ www.DenisWaitley.com

SHARON LECHTER ~ 5 Time N.Y. Times Best-Selling Author. Author of *Think and Grow Rich for Women*, Co-Author of *Exit Rich, Rich Dad Poor Dad, Three Feet from Gold, Outwitting the Devil* and *Success and Something Greater* ~ www.SharonLechter.com

JIM CATHCART~ Best-Selling Author of *Relationship Selling* and *The Acorn Principle,* among many others. Certified Speaking Professional (CSP) and Former President of the National Speakers Association (NSA) ~ www.Cathcart.com

STEVE SIMS ~ N.Y.Times Best-Selling Author of *Bluefishing - The Art of Making Things Happen,* CEO and Founder of Bluefish ~ www.SteveDSims.com

GLENN LUNDY ~ Husband to one, Father to 8, Automotive Industry Expert, Author of "The Morning 5", Creator of the popular morning show "#riseandgrind", and the Founder of "Breakfast With Champions" ~ www.GlennLundy.com

MARIE DIAMOND ~ Featured in *The Secret*, Modern Day Spiritual Teacher, Inspirational Speaker, Feng Shui Master ~ www.MarieDiamond.com

DAN CLARK ~ Award Winning Speaker, Speaker Hall of Fame, N.Y. Times Best-Selling Author of *The Art of Significance* ~ www.DanClark.com

ALEC STERN ~ America's Startup Success Expert, Co-Founder of Constant Contact, Speaker, Mentor, Investor ~ www.AlecSpeaks.com

ERIK SWANSON ~ 10 Time #1 International Best-Selling Author, Award Winning Speaker, Featured on Tedx Talks and Amazon Prime TV. Founder & CEO of the Habitude Warrior Brand ~ www.SpeakerErikSwanson.com

LORAL LANGEMEIER ~ 5 Time N.Y. Times Best-Selling Author, Featured in *The Secret*, Author of *The Millionaire Maker* and *YES! Energy - The Equation to Do Less, Make More* ~ www.LoralLangemeier.com

DORIA CORDOVA ~ CEO of Money & You, Excellerated Business School, Global Business Developer, Ambassador of New Education ~ www.FridaysWithDoria.com

JOHN ASSARAF ~ Chairman & CEO NeuroGym, MrNeuroGym.com, N. Y. Times best-selling author of *Having It All, Innercise,* and *The Answer.* Also featured in *The Secret* ~ www.JohnAssaraf.com

KEVIN HARRINGTON ~ Original "Shark" on the hit TV show *Shark Tank,* Creator of the Infomercial, Pioneer of the *As Seen on TV* brand, Co-Author of *Mentor to Millions* ~ www.KevinHarrington.TV

GRAB YOUR COPY OF AN OFFICIAL PUBLICATION
WITH THE ORIGINAL UNEDITED TEXT FROM 1937
BY THE NAPOLEON HILL FOUNDATION!

THE NAPOLEON HILL FOUNDATION
WWW.NAPHILL.ORG

Global Speakers Mastermind &
Habitude Warrior Masterminds

Join us and become a member of our tribe! Our Global Speakers Mastermind is a virtual group of amazing thinkers and leaders who meet twice a month. Sessions are designed to be 'to the point' and focused, while sharing fantastic techniques to grown your mindset as well as your pocket books. We also include famous guest speaker spots for our private Masterclasses. We also designate certain sessions for our members to mastermind with each other & counsel on the topics discussed in our previous Masterclasses. It's time for you to join a tribe who truly cares about **YOU** and your future and start surrounding yourself with the famous leaders and mentors of our time. It is time for you to up-level your life, businesses, and relationships.

For more information to check out our Masterminds:
Team@HabitudeWarrior.com
www.DecideTobeAwesome.com

BECOME AN INTERNATIONAL
#1 BEST-SELLING AUTHOR & SPEAKER

Habitude Warrior International has been highlighting award-winning Speakers and #1 Best-Selling Authors for over 25 years. They know what it takes to become #1 in your field and how to get the best exposure around the world. If you have ever considered giving yourself the GIFT of becoming a well-known Speaker and a fantastically well known #1 Best-Selling Author, then you should email their team right away to find out more information in how you can become involved. They have the best of the best when it comes to resources in achieving the best-selling status in your particular field. Start surrounding yourself with the N.Y. Times Best-Sellers of our time and start seeing your dreams become reality!

For more information to become a #1 Best-Selling Author & Speaker on our Habitude Warrior Conferences
Please send us your request to:
Team@HabitudeWarrior.com
www.DecideTobeAwesome.com